PUBLISHED BY RANDOM HOUSE CANADA

Kitten Clone is the third book in the Writers in Residence series, which was founded by Alain de Botton.

Library and Archives Canada Cataloguing in Publication

Coupland, Douglas, author
    Kitten clone : inside Alcatel-Lucent / Douglas Coupland.

Includes index.
Issued in print and electronic formats.

ISBN 978-0-345-81411-1

    1. Technology—Social aspects.
2. Technology—Psychological aspects. 3. Internet—Social aspects.
4. Internet—Psychological aspects.
5. Alcatel-Lucent (Firm). I. Title.

T14.5.C69 2014   303.48'3
C2013-908606-4

Typography: Chronicle & Knockout by Hoefler & Frere-Jones; Apercu by The Entente

Printed and bound in Canada

10 9 8 7 6 5 4 3 2 1

Kitten Clone
by Douglas Coupland

INSIDE ALCATEL-LUCENT

Random House Canada

Paris

Kitten Clone
by Douglas Coupland

Shanghai

New Jersey

Photographs by
Olivia Arthur

Introduction 9

Fugue 13
Belfort, France,
1871

Past 21
Berkeley Heights,
New Jersey, USA
Holmdel Township,
New Jersey, USA

Present 91
Paris, France
Calais, France
Kanata, Ontario,
Canada

Future 137
Pudong,
Shanghai,
China

Introduction

You're holding a book about a company you've most likely never heard of. This company has no Steve Jobs, nor does it have a CEO who jet-skis with starlets. It's only the 461st largest company on earth, but were it to vanish tomorrow, our modern world would immediately be the worse for its absence, with global communications severely crippled until its competitors swooped in to fill the void. Your home and office Internet would be slowed right down, if not stopped altogether. As we always learn during basic power failures, we'd be reminded yet again how utterly we depend on complex systems far beyond our reach or influence...

I'd never heard of Alcatel-Lucent, and once its existence was pointed out to me, it was still very, very hard to find—sort of like the cloud, whose existence Alcatel-Lucent (or "Alca-Loo" as it's known among financiers) both helped to create and helps to continue. Alcatel-Lucent played a crucial role in designing, building and maintaining the Internet. This book records my exploration of Alca-Loo in four locations where its presence is highly present—the United States, France, Canada and China.

This book also uses what I learned about Alca-Loo as a stepping stone into larger meditation... about what data and speed and optical wiring are doing to us as a species—about what the Internet is doing to us as it relentlessly colonizes the planet and our brains, about how a totally under-the-radar company has transformed our interior lives, and how far the process will go before people step back and say, "You know, I really don't remember my pre-Internet brain at all."

I could never have written this book had Alain de Botton not spent a week at Heathrow Airport and then used his experiences there as a way of musing on travel and the human soul in his book *A Week at the Airport*. His decision to expand his project by asking other writers to investigate other organizations made for a fascinating year. Thank you, Alain.

This book has a "surfy" feel to it. I wanted to mirror the way we look for information on the Internet: its random links, its chance encounters, and its happy coincidences. I trekked over three continents trying to locate the core of something that largely has no core, which led me to conclude that maybe it doesn't need one. From its beginnings as a tiny locomotive company in France's Alsace region in 1871, Alca-Loo has become a shapeless global beast. In it I discovered a company clearly divided into past, present and future. Its research division, Bell Labs, was both deeply funded and protected by the

American government; it gave us much of what defined the twentieth century: nearly all of our communication, computer and satellite systems. Alcatel-Lucent is justifiably proud of what Bell Labs has given mankind, yet at the same time it lives in Bell Labs' shadow, in a new Darwinian universe of decreased fundamental research funding, amorphous transnational leadership and crazy information technologies that logarithmically morph everything they touch into something new, unprecedented and challenging.

Of course, Alca-Loo's offices operate entirely in the present, in the moment-to-moment expediency required to deal with competitors, new technologies, politicians and stockholders. And then there is the Alca-Loo of the future: the Chinese government has mandated that by 2017 all Chinese citizens will get a minimum of 200 megs of data per second of Internet speed, and Alca-Loo's Shanghai branch is working on doing that.

I would be surprised if Alcatel-Lucent is still called Alcatel-Lucent in a decade. Such companies seem to always be shedding divisions, swapping DNA with other companies, selling off their bits and pieces, and they're always changing names. So the book is a screen-snap of 2013, our all-too-brief present—that may indicate new directions we might head toward.

When I started researching this book, I thought that the Internet was a metaphor for life; now I think life is a metaphor for the Internet. I'm not trying to be cute. Just as it is impossible to point to a single spark within the human brain that proves life, so it is impossible to disprove that the Internet is a living thing. It is massive. It never sleeps. And more and more, it's talking about us behind our backs.

Douglas Coupland,
January 2014

FUGUE

F
U
G
U
E

Belfort,
France.

The year is 1871. You are French and you are about to fondle a kitten.

To be more specific, your name is Alphonse Garreau and you are eighteen years old and it's your first day on the job as an ironmonger at a new locomotive works. You're in the town of Belfort, France, some ninety miles south of Strasbourg. Belfort is the capital of the Territoire de Belfort, a trading centre specializing in Alsatian wines, cereals and textiles—but heavy industry is now coming into play. You, Alphonse, have just been hired by the Société Alsacienne de Constructions Mécaniques, founded by industrialists who have defected from a firm a few miles upriver in Mulhouse, a place that was annexed by the Rhineland after last year's defeat in the Franco-Prussian war.

And while you, Alphonse, are walking to your first day on the new job, you see a crazy old woman doing something odd at the bottom of the stone steps to the Savoureuse, a slowly moving brandy-coloured river that cuts through the town's core. You go to investigate and find that the crone has a wicker basket that she is dunking in and out of the tea-stained water, and when you ask her why, she says she is drowning kittens she found in a nearby barn.

You're not an animal lover. Not so many people are—it will be several decades before the general populace undergoes the societal transformation that makes it sentimental about pets. But something about these particular kittens drowning strikes you as sad, so you ask the old woman if you could see them. Among four dead kittens, one remains alive, with black fur and white feet, like socks. You ask the crone if you can have it and she sticks out her hand, so you give her ten centimes. The kitten goes in your jacket pocket and you continue on your way to work.

Except now you realize you need to feed the cat something—but what? What on earth were you thinking, bringing a kitten on the first day of a new job?

Here's what you were thinking: you're no longer working on a farm. You're now a part of industry. You're going to make locomotives. You are working in the future. You are working in a region the newspaper has called "the Manchester of France." You feel like part of the future, and having new life in your pocket amplifies this sensation. But this new life requires milk.

Then, as you're passing a barn, you hear cows mooing, so you go over to have a look through the stable door... perfect. There's nobody inside, but you see a pail brimming with milk. All that milk just wait-

13

P

A

S

T

P

A

S

T

Holmdel
Township,
New Jersey,
USA

Berkeley
Heights,
New Jersey,
USA

The shuttle bus from the local hotel drops me off outside what appears to be an architecturally unmodified early-1980s facility for making robot housewives. Hot robot housewives. Hot corn-fed robot housewives who look like Ann-Margret in her prime. Housewives who spend their off-hours in sunless living rooms, their internal servers humming on PAUSE, blindly flipping back and forth through pages of old *Life* magazines that smell like a basement, their software awaiting the 6:30 a.m. release signal, when they will proceed upstairs to administer wake-up backrubs to their masters.

But I'm actually standing in front of Bell Laboratories—Bell Labs—a sprawling industrial research campus built of brick the colour of a wet golden Labrador, in the centre of suburban New Jersey's belt of once-utopian corporate campuses that began springing up here in the 1950s, the acme of the military industrial complex era. A pyramid-capped core building, maybe eight stories high, has two symmetrical wings that flank the central area and absorb what is clearly an older, 1940s utilitarian structure, visible at the complex's rear side, to the east. The oak trees here are big; maybe they were planted back then.

It's late February and the grass surrounding the complex is brown. The bus driver, who spends eight hours a day pinballing between corporate campuses, including L'Oréal, Sandoz, Ciba-Geigy and NCR (there's not enough population in the region to support a full-time local taxi), tells me there's been no snow this year. He tells me he hopes the absence of snow isn't thanks to human beings. "It's getting harder and harder not to believe in global warming, but I'm still going to keep on trying. I hope that whatever you're doing in that building isn't wrecking the snow." As he closes the door, he shouts, "You be good!"

The outside air is just above freezing, and it's humid. My lungs feel like bags of romaine lettuce forgotten in the fridge's crisper. Out by the main road there's a field of solar panels, but it's hard to imagine anything extracting energy out of a day like today.

I'm discombobulated this morning because I forgot my iPhone, so I have that homesick, disconnected feeling you get when you realize you're phoneless. I'm jet-lagged and I'm concerned because the date on the shuttle bus's dashboard clock reminded me that it's already February. Time is moving too quickly these days—and yet, at the same time, it's moving too slowly. And it's not just that I'm growing older. Quite simply, my brain no longer feels the way it used to; my sense of time is distinctly different from what it once was, and I miss my pre-Internet brain. The Internet has burrowed inside my head and laid eggs, and it feels like they're all hatching. Welcome to the early twenty-first century, a world where the future somehow feels like... homework.

Of course, I know that my perception of time's passage is not changing because of Internet eggs hatching inside my brain. What's really happening is that, after more than ten thousand hours of exposure to the Internet and digital technologies like my iPhone, my brain has been rewired—or, rather, it has rewired itself. Science has a name for this process: Hebb's Law. When neurons fire together, they wire together. It's no coincidence that the ten-thousand-hour rule has recently entered our culture's popular imagination, explaining to us that after doing something for ten thousand hours, you become an expert at it, because that's how much time your brain needs to fully rewire itself to adapt to a new medium.

Ask yourself if you've spent ten thousand hours on the Internet, then think about your own brain. It's clear there's a new neural reality. If you're in doubt, look at people younger than you. Do they interact with other people and the world differently than you did when you were their age? Of course they do. So, sometime between then and now, big changes have occurred. Our attention spans are collapsing: we want movies; we want music; we want unfiltered information. We want Season Four of *Dexter*. And we want it all now. Nearly omniscient levels of information are now cheaply available across pretty much all cultures and to most of the world's citizens. As a result, politics is changing. Religion is changing. Our sense of intuition is changing. The way we solve problems is changing. Everything is changing, and far too quickly to be absorbed, especially by people who lived in the 1970s, when the single biggest tech improvement over a decade was the addition of an FM dial to car radios, or people who lived in the 1980s when the single biggest tech upgrade was the ability to create a mixed-tape cassette for your girlfriend. Acceleration is accelerating.

I think of this while watching Bell Labs workers bustle into the building. They're mainly flowing up from the lower parking lot where they parked a fleet of silver, white and black sedans. Many are carrying briefcases and messenger bags containing laptops: these days you bring your own computer to work.

I enter through gold-tinted glass doors on the west side of the building, and the early-1980s fantasia continues. The high-ceilinged concrete space is filled with display cases filled with artifacts filled with

22

astonishing significance: the world's first transistor (1947); the world's first laser (1957); a replica of the world's first satellite (1961). A plasma TV displays in real time the current number of patents generated by the building's occupants: 29,002 as of this morning.

This place feels like the world's biggest dad's den. No, that's not quite right. It's more like... it's more like if you were shopping for vintage motherboards on Craigslist and you drove to an *E.T.*-style suburb and knocked on the garage door, where there's a rental suite, and a guy opens the door—his name is Gavin—and inside, Gavin is surrounded by his tech shrines: dust-free gaming consoles, a kendo sword in a special Japanese-made sword-holding rack, several autographed baseballs and maybe a few sci-fi figurines, and while his stuff is arguably quite cool, it's also very hard not to notice that Gavin doesn't have a girlfriend. Does that make sense?

So here I am in the lobby of a building filled with some of the coolest stuff in human history, in a massive Gavin-style space, and I'm trying to figure out how to hook the building up with a date—perhaps with the L'Oréal campus a few miles to the south.

I head to the desk to obtain my security badge. It's very dark in here: no bulb seems to have a higher wattage than 40, and half of them are switched off. While pinning on my badge, I look up. There, attached to a concrete rotunda above me, is a foam-core board bearing a lavender circle the size of a basketball hoop—it's the first springtime colour I've seen since entering the building. And inside the circle is... a protein molecule? A Japanese hiragana character? No, it's a corporate logo, an abstraction of our two friends, the letter "A" and the letter "L."

The "A" stands for Alcatel, and the "L" stands for Lucent.

Alcatel-Lucent owns Bell Labs.

Most of us have never heard of Alcatel-Lucent, but, essentially, it builds and maintains a huge chunk of the Internet. The company was formed in 2006 by the 25-billion-euro merger of France's Alcatel and the U.S. firm Lucent Technologies. It employs 80,000 people in 130 countries and has annual revenue of 16 billion euros. Alcatel-Lucent helps us transmit our voices, our movies and our data between landlines, mobile devices and the Internet. In this sense, it's a platform company: it doesn't provide content, it provides channels. You likely interact with Alcatel-Lucent hundreds of times a day without knowing it.

Alcatel's work is at the core of humanity's internal rewiring, as well as spin-off effects such as the Arab Spring and China's quasi-democracy.

23

Douglas Coupland

Alcatel is an embodiment of the new Western neural condition, and at the same time is its mirror. It is transnational, decentralized and emotionally neutral. It feeds on information, it has a perpetual urge to upgrade and it is always dissatisfied with the present. It exists purely to go forward. It demands and fosters ever more speed, and ever more information saturation and, especially, ever more networks.

In the days of Alphonse Garreau, people communicated across distance with church bells or sent each other paper missives by way of a postal service; if the need was urgent, there was the telegram, which still required a person to bring the message to your door. These days, we do it with networks. A network is not something you buy in a box. It is a sprawling, messy, planetary machine with countless interdependent parts. There's wire and fibre to carry traffic—enough optical fibre has been laid to circle the globe eleven thousand times—and there's an astonishing amount of highly unglamorous equipment and devices such as switches, routers and satellites overseen by governments and regulatory bodies—all so that you can look up the lyrics to Bon Jovi songs any time you want and then buy novelty smart phone ring tones on impulse.

Of course, a global network is not something out of science fiction that would run forever if people disappeared from the planet. The network needs millions of people to define it, build it, maintain it, manage it and adapt it to meet the ever-morphing demands of seven billion human beings—a number that is only growing. As I clip on my security badge, I consider the implications of that. How scary: seven billion calorie-hungry primates out there causing trouble. Sometimes I think maybe it's best that people spend so much time inside looking at screens; if they were out there in the physical world, they'd just be wrecking stuff. Our species now has a babysitter, and we're still trying to figure out just why it is that for an activity that's so intensely and utterly private—going online— its net effect is that of locating and amplifying allegiances to groups.

Fleetingly, I wonder if the Bell Labs building has free WiFi, but I wonder that wherever I go now. Fun fact: Starbucks has the world's largest Internet footprint. Another fun fact: the tar sands processing town of Fort McMurray, Alberta, (population 76,000) has a disproportionately male population, and it also has North America's highest video streaming rate per capita—all those dateless nights spent watching old *M*A*S*H* reruns, one supposes.

Passing through the Bell Labs security gate, I look up once again at the purple A L logo. How on earth does a company land a weird and hard-to-remember name like Alcatel-Lucent? The answer? Telecom firms are like those high-school biology class presentations on DNA and cell reproduction, except corporate genetics are more tangled than straightforward mitosis or meiosis. Corporations are endlessly growing, splitting, merging, shedding divisions, having children with cousins, feasting on the remains of dead corporations and marrying their sisters, as well as mutating while they gorge on banquet tables loaded with patents acquired during mergers. The "Al" in the Alcatel portion of the name is like corporate DNA, like a Hapsburg chin passed along through the years: those two letters come from Alphonse Garreau's 1871 employer, the Société ALsacienne de Constructions Mécaniques.

Like many corporations, Alcatel-Lucent is an alloy of multiple semi-under-the-radar companies melted together to form a gigantic under-the-radar company. How under the radar is Alcatel-Lucent? Imagine you are staying at a Hotel Intercontinental in, say, Jakarta, and you see a discreet sign on the way to the breakfast room that says ALCATEL-LUCENT MARIANAS TRENCH CABLE DEPLOYMENT MEET-'N'-GREET. You're curious and want to see the room and the people at the meet-'n'-greet. You walk around, trying to find the room, but somehow, whether through misdirection, deflection, or a sudden blow to the back of the skull, you never quite get there. None of the diversionary tactics used to prevent you from finding the room are traceable back to Alcatel-Lucent, yet somehow they have achieved their corporate goal of staying under the radar.

Okay, that's a ridiculous analogy. Or is it?

Alcatel-Lucent crosses borders and is pretty much everywhere—its geographical diffuseness and its vast transnational financing are metaphorical embodiments of the age we live in.

Alphonse Garreau's vision of global kittenry has taken us from Belfort, France, to Berkeley Heights, New Jersey, and to Bell Labs' main buildings, known to its staff as Murray Hill, a nod to its original home in Manhattan's Murray Hill neighbourhood. Bell Labs is one of the most fundamentally important scientific touchpoints of twentieth-century communications. Bell Labs' job throughout that century was to research and perfect a near-indestructible American telephone system. And to their credit, they did. They accomplished this task beneath a protetive monopolistic cloak provided by the U.S. government, who deemed communications research too valuable to be left to the free-market research and development system. Thus the military industrial complex!

When the Internet began, remember, it used phone lines, not the remarkable optical fibres we can no longer live without, which were invented... here at Bell Labs. So a discussion of the Internet and twenty-first-century communications starts here.

To be extremely specific, the Internet was born at 10:30 p.m. on the evening of October 29, 1969, when a computer at the University of California, Los Angeles, used the telephone system devised at Bell Labs to connect with another computer at the Stanford Research Institute in what had yet to become Silicon Valley. Since that fateful moment, and particularly in the past decade, we've come to live with Google, Facebook, YouTube, Amazon, eBay... yeah, yeah, yeah, we all know the list.

Most importantly, somewhere along the line, this new supertool we've created permanently morphed our collective interior lives.

< br >

Once inside the building proper, I meet Deb McGregor from the press department—a glamorous person from the school of Money-penny whose rock-hard fist it probably was that knocked you out cold in Jakarta.

Our schedule is tight. Deb takes me past a set of windows over-looking a courtyard area to the west, where an apple tree is dozing through the winter. She tells me the tree was grown from a cutting taken from Sir Isaac Newton's apple orchard. Its variety is the Pride of Kent. So this New Jersey tree is a descendant of the apple tree that dropped the apple that Newton saw falling, triggering the thoughts that became his theory of gravity. Newton dealt with planets and solar systems. What would he have made of the past two hundred years? Almost every invention of note stems not from knowledge of the vastness of the universe but from its opposite: from knowledge of what happens at the tiniest of levels, with bacteria, viruses, atoms, and their subcomponents of electrons, protons, neutrons, quarks and so forth. Newton would be furious to have missed out on such a good science party.

I enter the cafeteria.

< br >

26

A few years ago I was meeting someone for lunch at a downtown Vancouver hotel, and in its lobby there were maybe two hundred people filling out some kind of application form. My first thought was that they were all applying for a very desirable job, but when I looked more closely at the applicants, I couldn't imagine any one job they might all be going for. They were such a diverse group: bike couriers, bankers in Zegna suits, mothers with kids. Yet they definitely had something highly specific in common, some common trait. Finally, I asked a young woman with a backpack what was going on, and she said, "Jeopardy! We want to be contestants on the show!" That was when I figured out what these people all had in common: they were smart.

I mention this because, upon entering the Bell Labs cafeteria, I feel like I am back in that *Jeopardy!* lobby once more, except in this case, the intelligence factor has escalated logarithmically, and because of this, the tribal dress code is even more extreme and specific. I am now in the land of profound genius—truly gifted mathematicians, scientists and engineers—a land I've learned to identify over the years by its unyielding dress code: khakis, brightly coloured nylon lanyards, card swipes, off-brand button-down shirts that have been washed too many times, footwear chosen solely for comfort, reading glasses from Duane Reade. Basically, whatever wasn't in the laundry hamper that morning.

I grab a coffee and sit down to get my bearings. Three men in their mid-thirties at the table beside me are making hand gestures and ack-ack noises that I find impenetrable. Perhaps they're using three dimensions plus sound to express a mathematical theorem of some sort—for example, "Is the present moment physically distinct from the past and future, or is it merely an emergent property of consciousness?"

So I ask these gentlemen what they're discussing, and I'm told, "We're simulating the technically correct way to eat hot dogs if you want to win a hot dog eating competition. Everyone wants to beat Takeru Kobayashi's[1] record. He's like a god." Okay, then: this is just the sort of problem scientifically gifted people take and solve, and then they extrapolate what they learned from the process and

---

1   Takeru Kobayashi (小林尊 Kobayashi Takeru) (born March 15, 1978) is a Japanese competitive eater. He held the world record for hot dog eating for nearly six years, and holds several other eating records, including four Guinness Records for hot dogs, meatballs, Twinkies, hamburgers, and pasta.

Douglas Coupland

convert the knowledge into a useful project. Bell Labs hires, literally, the smartest people on earth, about 25 percent from the United States, the remainder from Europe, Asia and the Indian subcontinent.

I wonder what sorts of projects these competitive fellows are working on. Perhaps they work in quantum computing, a field of research Bell Labs is actively engaged in. The quantum computer is a device that is still in its theoretical phase that makes direct use of quantum mechanical phenomena, such as superposition and entanglement, to perform operations on data. The difference between quantum computers and digital computers is based on transistors. Whereas digital computers require data to be encoded into binary digits (bits), quantum computation utilizes quantum properties to represent data and perform operations on these data. A theoretical model is the quantum Turing machine, also known as the universal quantum computer. Quantum computers share theoretical similarities with non-deterministic and probabilistic computers, like the ability to be in more than one state simultaneously. The field of quantum computing was first introduced by Richard Feynman in 1982. Although quantum computing is still in its infancy, experiments have been carried out in which quantum computational operations were executed on a very small number of qubits (quantum bits). Both practical and theoretical research continues, and many national government and military funding agencies support quantum computing research to develop quantum computers for both civilian and national security purposes, such as cryptanalysis. Large-scale quantum computers could be able to solve certain problems much faster than any classical computer by using the best currently known algorithms, like integer factorization using Shor's algorithm or the simulation of quantum many-body systems. There exist quantum algorithms, such as Simon's algorithm, which run faster than any possible probabilistic classical algorithm. Given unlimited resources, a classical computer can simulate an arbitrary quantum algorithm, so quantum computation does not violate the Church–Turing thesis. However, in practice infinite resources are never available and the computational basis of 500 qubits, for example, would already be too large to be represented on a classical computer because it would require two complex values to be stored. (For comparison, a terabyte of digital information stores only two discrete on/off values) Nielsen and Chuang point out that "trying to store all these complex numbers would not be possible on any conceivable classical computer." A classical computer has a memory made up of bits, where each bit represents either a one or a zero. A quantum computer maintains a sequence of qubits. A single qubit can represent a one, a zero, or, crucially, any quantum superposition of these two qubit states; moreover, a pair of qubits can be in any quantum superposition of 4 states, and three qubits in any superposition of 8. In general a quantum computer with n qubits can be in an arbitrary superposition of up to 2n different states simultaneously (this compares to a normal computer that can only be in one of these 2n states at any one time). A quantum number of qubits is fundamentally different from a classical computer composed of the same number of classical bits. For example, to represent the state of an n-qubit system on a classical computer would require the storage of 2n complex coefficients. Although this fact may seem to indicate that qubits can hold exponentially more information than their classical counterparts, care must be taken not to overlook the fact that the qubits are only in a probabilistic superposition of all of their states. This means that when the final state of the qubits is measured, they will only be found in one of the possible configurations they were in before measurement. Moreover, it is

I guess the point here is to not even try to enter the Himalayas of these Bell Labs minds. You'll die of intelligence depletion before you're even a few minutes out of base camp. Or stupidity poisoning. Or you'll just be left behind to die, and you'll have deserved it.

But there's something to consider here when thinking about intelligence and inventiveness, the two traits that best define Bell Labs. I offer the example of Bill Gates, the richest guy on earth, who's best friends with the other richest guys on earth, who are also the most intelligent guys on earth. So you have these fantastically rich and intelligent guys (no girls) going off on wilderness retreats and trying to blue-sky about what technologies are going to come down the pipe that they can create, own and manipulate. And what happens? These guys don't invent Google, and they don't invent Facebook, and they don't invent whatever comes next, because invention doesn't happen that way. Invention happens where and when it happens; you can't force invention into existence.

Looking at human history and the history of technology, there's a certain sort of inevitability to its parade. The wheel was going to be created sooner or later. Einstein developed the Special Theory of Relativity in 1905, but by 1910 someone else might have done so. Atomic energy; Velcro; search engines... they all would have been invented one way or another. The next society-changing technology is currently hurtling at us like a meteor, and there's zilch we can do to stop it.

This notion that humans exist only to propagate ever-newer technologies, that we are merely what Marshall McLuhan called "the sex organs of technology," is called technological determinism.

Depressing.

Or is technological determinism nonsense? Maybe we can control what we invent and when we invent it. Since 1925, Bell Labs has generated seven Nobel prizes and changed the course of humanity with stunning regularity. No California redwood forest full of brainstorming genius billionaires could compete with Bell Labs' creative heyday of the mid-twentieth century: the transistor, information theory, lasers, solar energy, radio astronomy, microchips, UNIX, mobile phones, mobile networks—all invented here. Most of these inventions led to the Internet in one way or other, and many of them could plausibly only have been invented here, in the way they were. So much for technological determinism.

And now the French own Bell Labs, which is a reasonably good thing, because being owned by Americans wasn't doing Bell Labs much

good. Bell Labs had been part of AT&T, which in 1984 was broken up as a result of an antitrust suit. In 1996 Bell Labs was spun off as part of Lucent Technologies, a 1990s dream stock that went from $7.56 to $84 in four years, only to be nearly destroyed by the 2001 telecom crash (a.k.a. "the overcapacity bubble"). The stock hit 55 cents a share in 2002.

The telecom crash happened six months after the dot-com crash of 2000 and, though it's less well known, caused the evaporation of two trillion dollars' worth of wealth. Four years later, Lucent Technologies was sold to the French telecommunications conglomerate Alcatel. Since then, the buildings of Murray Hill have been under a massive bell jar in which time has gone static, and there is the distinct sense here of being, if not embalmed, trapped in the past. There's not enough money to buy replacement light bulbs let alone fund massive fundamental research. Bell Labs of today is charged with creating an astonishing new future in a time-stand-still physical environment reminiscent of the hallways through which that small child raced his plastic scooter in *The Shining*.

31   < br >

The glamorous Deb McGregor takes me on an elevator from the cafeteria to a fourth-floor office that's a flawless hybrid of neutrality and casual neglect. There is sun-faded oatmeal carpeting in a state I don't normally even notice—unvacuumedness—floral prints bleached almost invisible by three decades of afternoon sun, empty recycling bins and more dust. It's actually kind of spooky, like somewhere your dad would hole up when your parents get divorced, minus Zantac bottles on the kitchen counter and the unused Soloflex workout machine rusting in front of the TV.

It's becoming clear to me that the building I am in no longer exists in the present tense. This is a building that has already happened. It is a building trapped in the past... or perhaps merely hypnotized by the past.

Whiteboards on the wall are covered with oak panels on dried-out hinges. Only every other pot light in the ceiling has a working bulb. I expect to find a stack of cassette boxes, also sun-faded and barely legible: MC Hammer; Missing Persons; Adam and the Ants. Five for a dollar, ten bucks for the whole box.

A circular table at the front of the room has four chairs and an antiquated conference-call box in the centre. This may be a tech environment, but it is definitely not Silicon Valley—certainly not the Valley of the 1990s where tech firms flaunted brightly coloured floor-to-floor slides, a pizza chef in the lobby, and a bouncy castle in the rear parking lot for the high-level coders with social phobias. This is a place that seems like it was once very elegant but then had some kind of stroke and just sort of... stopped.

I'm deeply gratified to find out that this office does not belong to Markus Hofmann, head of Bell Labs Research. Hofmann is a cheerful man in his late fifties who tells me that the office we're in belongs to nobody. "We don't really go for offices here in Bell Labs admin. Your office is basically wherever you are," he says. "We use whatever one is empty." In my mind, I rifle through magazine articles from the early 1990s that promised the dream of telecommuting, and how ridiculous and impossible it seemed, and how telecommuting has become one of the ambiguous answered prayers of our era: the good thing about always being connected is that you're always connected. But the downside of being connected is that you're always connected. Internet, you are one woeful and perplexing minx.

Hofmann, still a competitive water polo player, has spent thirteen years at Bell Labs. He hails from Germany and has a Ph.D. in computer engineering and a master's in computer science, both from the University of Karlsruhe. He is highly involved with the IEEE (pronounced I-triple-E, the Institute of Electrical and Electronics Engineers), a professional technological association headquartered in New York City.

He looks like a school principal who'd discipline you without resorting to corporal punishment, and his eyes tell me that, at any given moment he's probably figuring out the natural logarithm of his Visa card number or what his lunch might look like connected by strings into the fifth and/or sixth dimensions.

Hofmann tells me that the company's administration practices what it preaches. "We create global communication systems, and we use all of them ourselves." I mention that the nomadic existence of the Alca-Loo staffer is certainly different from Microsoft's eighty-hour-a-week staff being ball-and-chained to a Douglas fir tree in Washington State. Hofmann smiles. I look at the desk, where I notice a Trump Taj Mahal pen that reminds me I'm in New Jersey. I ask Hofmann what Bell Labs is currently working on and how it fits into Alcatel-Lucent.

"Bell Labs is a toolbox. Every day we ask ourselves: What do we want to build? And we can ask this knowing that what we build will

have real world deployment through Alcatel-Lucent."

Just then, there's a knock on the door, which is slightly annoying because I'm trying to hear what Hofmann is saying. I go to open it, and it's Alphonse Garreau. Quoi?!

"Bonjour, c'est moi, Alphonse. Je voudrais discuter de mon chaton."

"Alphonse, go away. This is no time to talk about your kitten."

"Pas même pour un peu?"

"No, not even for a bit. Au revoir, Alphonse."

I slam the door. Hofmann asks, "Don't tell me: that annoying French ghost again? The one who's always talking about his cat?"

"Oui."

"He won't leave us alone. He's like some kid who doesn't know the right night for trick-or-treating."

"What were we talking about?"

"We were discussing real-world deployment of inventions discovered here at Bell Labs and Alcatel-Lucent. Hey, wait a second, Doug—do you speak French?"

"Only really terrible Canadian high-school French. Any time you see me writing in French, it's merely English that's been run through Google Translate."

"I see. I wonder... how would you explain Google Translate to someone from 1871?"

"That's a good question. How would you even explain Google to someone from 1971? It's strange—if technologies are so inevitable, then why is the future so hard to predict?"

"How do you mean?" asks Hofmann.

"Take the iPhone. Now that it's here, it seems like it's been here forever and was utterly inevitable. And yet, if you scour books and movies since the late nineteenth century, even science fiction, you find few devices that resemble the iPhone.[2, 3] To the extent that I've worked on a few futurological panels in my life, even if you stick a big bunch of pretty forward-looking people in a room with delicious food and drink for a few days, visualizing the future is still crazy hard."

"You mean flying cars and that?"

"No. Not flying cars. The thing about the future is that it's not too different from right now—in fact, it's boringly very much like the present. Most of the buildings you see around you now are still around. Nature doesn't change much, though global warming makes me curious to see if there will be cacti in the Canadian Arctic in a century. People don't change much, either—except maybe in lifespan, health and proportions. People from a century ago would be amazed at how old the twenty-first-century populace is. Changes tend to be subtle: unusual new pets; unexpected cleaning products; noise levels (is the future noisier or quieter than right now?); higher protein intake; water bottles everywhere. Someone from forty years ago would be shocked to see how many varieties of mushroom are now carried at the local Safeway. That's the kind of change that really happens."

"What's the hardest thing about the future to predict?"

"That's easy. Transportation. Nobody has a clue what roads will look like in one or two hundred years, least of all automakers. It's because no one knows how quickly we'll gobble up what energy resources remain to us now, or where energy will come from.[4] And try as we might, it's far too early in our species' development to plausibly imagine teleportation beams transferring us from A to B."

"That's for sure."

"I've found that scientists are actually the last people you should ask about the future. I can't believe you and I have even gotten this far into the discussion. I've noticed that the moment you approach the point in a conversation when you might ask scientists to make a prediction, their bodies start to clench. And when you actually ask them to predict the future, they freeze completely, then say, 'No, I can't do that for you.'"

"So, Doug, do you believe in technological determinism?"

"I'm unsure. Bell Labs is making me feel differently about it."

"How so?"

35

2   In the *Star Trek* universe, a tricorder is a multifunctional hand-held device used for sensor scanning, data analysis and recording data.

3   Genuine fun fact: in 1992 when I handed in a manuscript, I was reprimanded by the editor for using a fax as part of the plot. "Not everyone can afford a fax machine, and including it here seems elitist and unfair to readers who can't be expected to either afford or understand what a fax machine is." In general, I try to include up-to-date technology in novels. Rather than dating them, it time codes them. People picking up, say, Microserfs, two decades later enjoy the book for its tech fidelity as for anything else.

4   The one appalling thing about electric cars is that one plugs them into already overtaxed municipal power grids. Try mentioning this to a politician or manufacturer who wants to ride the green wave and you will quickly find yourself escorted out of the room. Mention this twice and you'll magically find yourself on the No Fly List. Mention this three times and your cold lifeless body will be found in a clump of brambles off the nearest motorway.

"Well, you guys are an industrial research laboratory, right?"

"Yes. And we have Bell Labs in eight locations around the planet, not just here."

"Your job has always been to do research that furthers the future of communication. First for AT&T and the North American telephone monopoly, and then for Alcatel-Lucent."

"More or less. We do defence and aerospace research, too. We were founded in 1925, and we had labs in Manhattan, on the Lower West Side. The war was a huge boom time for us, and by 1947 we'd grown and had mostly moved out here to New Jersey. This location was one of three in the state, and is currently the HQ for Bell Labs."

"Okay, so as an industrial lab, your job is to be practical."

"Yes. But part of the success of Bell Labs has always been to marry abstract and fundamental research with the practical."

"Go on."

"In fact, the very structure of the labs here was meant to force communication between disciplines. The laboratory hallways are each one-eighth of a mile long and extremely narrow. Mervin Kelly, the man who designed the facility, deliberately assigned offices to scientists and mathematicians mixed in with electrical engineers, metallurgists, and other practical disciplines. You couldn't go for coffee without bumping into someone in the narrow halls, and staff members were encouraged to discuss their projects openly with one another. That's how the transistor came about in 1947—metallurgists having coffee with electronic engineers. But, Doug, I asked you about technological determinism."

"My thinking is that you can't rely on inventions to just happen on their own somewhere, and you can't rely on them to happen by accident. New inventions emerge because they're built on top of a layer of all previous inventions. And new inventions are far more likely to occur when two or more previously unassociated ideas are married together and produce offspring. You can consciously invent what comes next; you can determine the direction of a culture. Invention need not be a cosmic gift from the gods—although Einstein may have been a true gift."

"Hmmm," says Hofmann. "The transistor was invented here because vacuum tubes were too expensive and died too easily. But we couldn't have done anything too practical with the transistor unless someone figured out that information needs to be converted into ones and zeroes to be processed properly. That happened here, and was shared with the world in the July and October 1948 issues of the Bell System Technical Journal, in Claude Shannon's seminal 'A Mathematical Theory of Communication.' In the next decades, lasers and optical fibre were developed to overcome the limitations of copper wiring; cellular-based wireless communication was developed to maximize the amount of information that could be passed within a system. An iPhone 4, if made with vacuum tubes, would fill one-quarter of the Grand Canyon."

"Really?"

"No. I just made that up. I think it would be more like a fifty-foot cube, but that's not very interesting."

Suddenly a hand shakes my shoulder and I hear a voice with a faint German accent. "Doug, wake up. Wake up. Doug, I think you had a stroke or something. Do you want some water?"

Huh? What? I look up. Hofmann is looking at me from across the table.

"I think you fell asleep. We were talking about real-world deployment times."

"Right. Oh. Sorry. I'm jet-lagged. Deployment times. Right. Please continue."

Hofmann seems unfazed by my brief reverie. "Some people say the era of the big lab is over, but we don't. The pressure is on Bell Labs to do the big things again. Incremental development doesn't work anymore."

I'm unsure if this is true, as every day I find myself assaulted by endless new technologies, but what Hofmann is talking about is a radical new technology that obliterates everything that came before it, the way the transistor did.

Hofmann continues, "This is good, because it means that pure research is coming back. Fundamental research that creates entirely new ways of doing things."

I stare at the door cautiously, waiting for a knock.

Hofmann continues. "But finding out how and where to spend the pure research dollar is key. We can't merely react to things. We have to drive them. With some technologies, we're approaching the Shannon limit—the physical limit of wireless chip sizes. But even then binary computation has limitations."

Hofmann has kicked into that smartness warp I mentioned earlier. By computation limits, he's referring to the amount of ON-OFF information it's possible to process given the physical limitations of the atom.

I'm just smiling and nodding.

He continues, "So until there's a fundamental new way of doing things, we're going to have to test the limits of b a n d w i d t h. How we use bandwidth right now is wasteful. There are certain gains that can be made simply by more smartly allocating how the spectrum gets used. Nobody expected your thirteen-year-old daughter to want to watch high-res vampire movies on a hand-held mobile device while waiting for a bus. But that's what human beings want, and that's what human beings need." Hofmann looks out the window and then back at me. "The Internet surprised us with its mass adoption. We didn't see that one coming."

I ask, "Where do you see communications going in the future?"

"I think 'reachability' is the new dictum in our lives. We didn't expect the need for people to connect to each other to be so big."[5]

This is taking a second to sink in. After a pause, I ask, "Anything else?"

"Yes, battery life is a huge issue, in terms of both function and the environment. Bell Labs is on this in a major way, to reduce energy use by a factor of one thousand."

I ask him what he thinks the long-term effect of access to so much information is going to be.

"Currently, all Bell Labs staff members remember the pre-digital world; our ideal remains a hand-held plus a pen and paper. But that's us. Obviously, we're seeing more and more smart young people absorbing massive amounts of information, and we're unsure what the long-term effects will be."

I mention my theory of "omniscience fatigue." Thanks to Google and Wikipedia, for the first time in the history of humanity, it's possible to find the answer to almost any question, and the net effect of this is that information became slightly boring. (We have to face the fact that God might actually be bored by knowing all the answers to everything.)

Hofmann gives a dry chuckle. "We need deep, solid foundations

---

5   I must admit, I'm also surprised at how much human beings want to communicate with each other. But then again, for a process that's so intrinsically social, it's astonishing how isolating the online experience is. Would you ever dream of phoning a friend to say, "Hey, come on over to my house and we'll go online together!" No. No you would not. I rest my case.

and deep thinking to reach our next human level," he says. "Yet time is now the ultimate consideration. You can't go deep and solid without giving ideas time. But manufacturing competition is crazy, and we have such quick feedback now."

This schizoid new future doesn't seem to disturb Hofmann. His enthusiasm says that he's more than willing to face it head-on.

I think of my belief that we're entering a world without margins—a world composed of a global monoclass, with each citizen unit having the same fountain of information available regardless of place or culture. Andy Warhol believed that all the Chinese restaurants in Manhattan had just one jumbo kitchen underground that they all got their food from. In a way, our species' collective memory is now not unlike Warhol's Chinese kitchen. We all get our information from the same kitchen and there's just one menu and it's called "The Same Internet for Everyone on Earth." So give a yak herder in rural Tibet some smooth connectivity and he'll access the same memory menu you do, and instead of going to yaks.com, he's probably going to kill time reading the really scary and bitter one-star hotel reviews on Tripadvisor.com—or maybe he'll get caught in a cute puppy warp on YouTube or maybe he'll make himself a worthier person by bingeing on TED talks but, to be honest, he'll probably be checking out porn. So. Much. Porn.

Hofmann continues, "We have to consider the impact of a technology, its time to market, and its process. Is the company pursuing too many near-term projects? Are we overestimating their impact? How much should you spend on internal research, as opposed to buying new technologies? Prioritizing ideas is crucial."

Suddenly there really is a knock on the door, and my blood chills: Another ghost? But no, it's Deb to escort me to my next stop.

I thank Hofmann and re-enter the dusty, dark, sound-muffled hallway graced with an occasional underwatered, light-starved tropical plant. I see a water fountain, but I eye its dusty stainless steel surface with suspicion: there is a good chance nobody has drunk from that fountain in decades. Yet I am thirsty. Dare I drink? I go for it, and the water that trickles out is slightly warmer than room temperature—no healing Pool of Bethesda, this. This is water that somehow manages to taste... dry. Mummified water. Oh, dear God, I am drinking undead tap water. But it's too late. I can feel the water entering my bloodstream, colonizing my body, the way latex fills blood vessels and organs in those creepy human anatomy displays.

Douglas Coupland

I'm imagining my latex-mummified body at the local science centre, being photographed by millions of iPhones owned by millions of bored teenagers on fieldtrips—teens who are much more sensibly interested in sex, rather than my latexed carcass. My body will be looking at them all, texting each other—sexting each other. These children who learned how to deactivate Google's SafeSearch option the same afternoon they learned how to teeter-totter. Detentions for everybody!

And even from the vantage point of latexed death, I know the photos of my corpse will be only grudgingly pasted into Facebook, or whatever technology eats up Facebook, and they will never once be liked or favourited, or accessed again, except briefly, millennia in the future, when a team of resonance scanning bots scour excavated twenty-first-century landfills in pursuit of some nugget of data that will allow them to find an antidote to New Jersey tap water strain NC078-D, a nanolife form that renders humans unable to program the time setting of their microwave ovens.

And then... *blink* ... I am delivered back to the present. Phew.

Strangely refreshed, I follow Deb down another dusty, muffled hallway that looks about to bust out into a Corey Hart video at any moment: the absence of light pretty much demands choreography that incorporates clever slatted shadows from venetian blinds.

But why is this place so dark? I look at the power outlets along the walls—maybe they could add a few standing lamps to brighten things up a bit. I then find an outlet and stare at it briefly: two little frozen screams, one atop the other, each horrified by the disaster they've brought to the world.

During the Depression, when electrical power was introduced into the American south, rural folk looked at electrical outlets with fear and distrust, imagining electricity as a malignant force, neither alive nor dead, oozing out of the pronged slots and into their homes. To counteract this fear, the hydroelectric industry invented the character Reddy Kilowatt, a simple, very likeable fellow made of lightning bolts, with a face that presaged the smiley face of the 1960s. Reddy Kilowatt made it clear that electricity comes from a happy, man-made place, not from a scary spirit world.

Who is the Reddy Kilowatt of our era? Google. It's a cartoon character because it's just so darn fun to say: Google! Google! Google! How could something called Google be unfriendly? And if Google was able to seduce my seventy-something parents into going online, then Reddy, hand over your lightning bolt, there's a new kid in town.

Bob running from the paparazzi--again

A century ago, electricity went from being something sinister, administered by that walrus-mustached guy from the Monopoly board, to being something invisible yet benign. Likewise, computing power is transitioning from being a grossly overpriced and overpackaged set of cables, software, and bulky hardware, overlorded by a combination of Bill Gates, Jeff Bezos and Sailor Moon, to being a vapory blankness that's "out there somewhere": the cloud

cloud

cloud

cloud

cloud

cloud

cloud.

Computing is all too rapidly becoming a utility—complex, surprisingly mundane, and blank—best administered by engineers, who probably pity your inability to program your microwave oven's time feature.

Can you imagine opening a newspaper and reading an article in the business section titled "Improve Your Productivity with 105-Volt AC Power"? Of course not. And the day will shortly be here when a business article titled "Use Computing to Boost Your Productivity" will seem equally pointless.

Computing is becoming as cheap and quick as electricity. Farewell, corporate mainframe. Farewell, office hard drive. Farewell, home hard drive. Farewell to that Rubbermaid tub out in the garage filled with its toxic linguini of power cords, adaptor cords, adaptors, battery cords, batteries, chargers and extension cords. We are now in the adolescence of the creation of a global information grid with near universal access.

This is good news for Alcatel-Lucent, as it means lots and lots of data zipping about the planet. In the telecom bubble of the late 1990s, before the crash of 2001, the world's telecom firms, amid stratospheric stock market expectations, built a glorious global optical fibre network. Unfortunately, they built it in an era when there was little data to send. They created eight-lane, flawlessly paved, immaculately decorated freeways when people were still driving horse-drawn buggies. A decade later, two billion people are online, and while most of us drive limping old Model Ts, soon enough we'll have Ferraris—and soon enough after that, this metaphor will collapse.[6] That is our real future, one largely driven by your thirteen-year-old daughter's need to watch *Twilight* sequels in HD on the school bus.

< br >

Deb has changed the order of my appointments at Bell Labs, and takes me from the dusty, underlit hallways into the icy world outside, across the large, noble front lawn to a windowless brick building about three stories tall. In the process, the sequence of events I'd planned for the day is shattered.

Sequencing is a funny activity almost entirely unique to human beings. Some crows have been shown to sequence, but dogs, while highly intelligent, cannot form sequences; it's the reason well-trained pups at dog shows are led from station to station by handlers instead of completing the course themselves.

Humans are entirely sequential thinkers. Some people can jump from task to task to task very quickly and give the semblance of simultaneous thinking, but this is an illusion; we remain serial thinkers.

It's ironic that the world of computer programming, possibly the most necessarily linear of all human pursuits, creates products that turn people into increasingly nonlinear thinkers. The people we most associate with buzzy, pseudo-simultaneous wired thinking are jabber-fingered video gamers—or maybe those drone operators in Virginia who bomb small middle villages in the Afghan hills while they snack on bar mix and 7 Up. Sometimes I wonder if the only skill we learn from playing video games is the ability to play more video games. There exists in our society the urban legend of the crazed game wizard who can burn through all levels of *Diablo III* in two hours, and how he goes on to become a jet-fighter pilot, his wits honed by two decades in the basement, drinking Pepsi and eating ramen noodles. In fact, the Air Force only wants physically fit, highly rational, icily

58

6   *Sigh.* I remember the early 1990s when everyone used the term "information superhighway" with straight faces. And in the end it turned out to be a cloud.

even-tempered pilots. I don't think anything would get you ejected from the Air Force jet-fighter training program faster than to say, "Wow, this is just like *Battlefield 3: Wake Island!*"

The larger point here is that the sequences we experience in our lives have become progressively shorter, more numerous and more disjointed over the past hundred years, from twelve-hour books to one-hour radio dramas to thirty-second TV commercials to four-frame animated GIFs to five ammo blasts per second. Some workplace studies have shown that humans prefer to change tasks roughly every two and a half minutes, or the length of one Beatles song (a vein of thinking that might be countered with a terse, "So, then, explain why everyone also loves 'Stairway to Heaven'" and binge-watching their favourite TV series.)

Inside the brick building, we enter a small, cold, neutral office space, furnished indifferently, where I meet a middle-aged man named Gary, who is blowing up a brightly coloured birthday party balloon. This is odd, but then what's wrong with odd? Sometimes, as Internet browsing has taught us all, a nice hit of oddness is just the ticket, that Wikipedia search on vitamin B that devolved into a two-hour marathon of Parkour fails or visits to the quilt archives of American Midwest museums—or, like the lonely men of Fort McMurray, Alberta, into countless solo hours of *M*A*S*H* reruns.

Randomness and unexpected hits of information have the effect of breaking us out of our too-linear thinking—and our overly rapid thinking. And one can't help but wonder about this overabundance of rapid sequencing from the Internet and its effect on our internal rhythms; the constant jostle between work and diversion, between diversion and friends and family and so on. The opposite of this jostle is possibly the reading of books—fiction—a highly focused leisure-based activity. Reading inculcates in readers a strong sense of individualism. The act of reading gave the world, for a few centuries or so, a society composed of "individuals." The Internet as a medium, however, has imbued most of us with the feeling of being one among many—seven billion, to be correct. If reading books made us long for our lives to be stories, the Internet has changed our lives into a mere series of tasks performed in a sequence. The narrative flow of our lives has somehow been stripped away.

The now fading notion that our lives should be stories is a psychological inevitability imbued in readers by the logic of the book and fiction as a medium: focus; sequencing; emotional through-lines; morals; structure; climax; dénouement. One can look back on the print era and witness true poignancy: readers the world over were determined to see their lives as stories, when, in fact, books are a specific invention that creates a specific mindset. Most people can't find the larger story in their lives. Born, grew up, had kids, maybe, and died... what kind of story is that? There's a maxim in the world of urban planning that if you let your city be planned by bakers, you will end up with a city of bakeries. If you have a culture whose brains are "planned" by books, you'll have a citizenry who want their lives to be book-like. If you have a culture whose brains are "planned" by digital culture and Internet browsing, you'll have a citizenry who want their lives to be simultaneous, fluid, ready to jump from link to link—a society that assumes that knowledge is there for the asking when you need it. This is a very different society from one peopled by book readers.[7]

Yet the residual need for one's life to be a story persists from the print era, especially in people born before 1970. Print era holdouts see the nonlinear children of the web as shallow and emotionally impoverished. Young people "born digital," with no vested emotional engagement with books, view print holdouts as souls adrift in a useless sea of nostalgia.

But we were talking about balloons, weren't we? Yes, a man named Gary is inflating coloured party balloons: three of them. He explains that the door beside us leads to the anechoic chamber, or soundproof room: the quietest place on the planet. While Gary inflates his three balloons, I will allow the Internet to tell you:

> *The Murray Hill anechoic chamber, built in 1940, is the world's oldest wedge-based anechoic chamber. The interior room measures approximately 30 feet high by 28 feet wide by 32 feet deep. The exterior cement and brick walls are about 3 feet thick to keep outside noise from entering the chamber.*

7   For Westerners, this loss of narrative can feel like a big step down, but for those from other cultures, entrance into the Internet's world of distraction is big step up, as one can now feel like a member of the global dinner conversation. And who's to say any of this is wrong or right? Being a "narrative" individual is maybe overrated. Some scientists believe that individualism may, in fact, be a form of brain mutation not evenly spread throughout the population, a mutation that poses a threat to those not possessing it. The cult of individuality may, in fact, prove to be a misguided genetic fallacy.

The name "anechoic" literally means "without echo." Large fibreglass wedges mounted on the interior surfaces of the chamber absorb echoes or reflections. The wedge-shaped absorbers are 4.5 feet long and 2 feet square at the base. Most current anechoic chambers utilize the alternating wedge pattern that was first used in the Murray Hill chamber. The chamber absorbs over 99.995% of the incident acoustic energy above 200 Hz.[8]

Gary fills the third balloon and twists its end. He then quickly holds it up to my face and pops it.

What the hell?

He tells me there's a reason he did that—just hang in there. So I do. Gary then opens what turns out to be a three-foot-thick door that would be the envy of any Austrian gentleman with a yen for DIY basement prison cells. I enter a cube surfaced with incredibly dusty wedges (unvacuumed since 1940), lit with more low-wattage bulbs. Gary follows with his two remaining balloons and closes the door behind him. We walk across a wire grate that takes us to the cube's geometrical centre. There is no sound. None. It's a dream! No, even better—it's a dream within a dream.

I want to live here.

Gary says, "Watch this," then pops another balloon. The popping makes almost no sound—about as much as a business card falling onto a tabletop. I really wasn't expecting that. Gary says, "That's how much noise a popped balloon makes. What you perceive as a pop is actually what we call its sonic skeleton."

I reply, "There's a term for you."

"Now watch me pop another balloon," Gary says. I do, and then he asks me, "Do you know what was different with that last pop?" I say no. "Your face didn't flinch. You knew there wasn't going to be a loud noise."

He is correct. But why have an anechoic chamber in the first place?

Gary tells me. "We use it to measure the sound ratings for industrial equipment. As well, opera companies have taped singers singing here to keep a baseline copy of their voices for the records. We can compare that baseline recording with live and recorded situations to understand just how much the opera hall's acoustics and the recording studio have modified an artist's voice."

8   A salad of data created from both Wikipedia and Alcatel-Lucent's website.

Douglas Coupland

I note a pile of popped balloons on the floor in the centre of the room, and at this moment I begin to have a minor crisis of faith, because what on earth does this room, or mummified tap water, or dust and dead light bulbs have to do with Alcatel-Lucent or the Internet or the twenty-first century or… or anything? Why on earth am I in suburban New Jersey—amid a world of stately homes and pharmaceutical manufacturers yo-yoing in and out of industry down cycles? I mean, the Internet is truly, really, honestly not a very glamorous place, and in many ways is utterly un-complex, but at least it is of the moment and not lost in time like Bell Labs seems to be.

What is the Internet, really? Breaking it down: your home computer is connected by copper wires and optical fibre to huge rooms, most likely in New York or London, filled with machines called routers that direct your request to Google or a university server or campbellsoup.com or whipkittensinbondage.net or wherever. Data tends to be stored in massive Stalag-like data farms (a.k.a. the cloud) located in remote, cool, dry places or places with lots of cheap energy. And then the process is reversed when the data you requested goes back to you.

That's it.

It's hard to imagine Matt Damon being cast in Internet: The Movie. And yet…

And yet Deb McGregor is in charge, and there's no time for vexing, free-floating anxiety. There is the world of ideas, and then there is the world itself, and now we're to head back to the main building by way of the solar farm.

In farewell, Gary says, "I bet you're going to use the balloons as a metaphor for the industry."

I wonder: Will I?

< br >

Solar farm. I know. The very words conjure up images of Paul and Linda McCartney not eating meat in a stone house on some godforsaken Scottish island where it's always raining and sheep covered in dung dreads huddle beneath the front door portico. On the roof, there's a solar panel the size of a cardboard box that generates just enough energy to fuel preteen Stella's first crimping iron, which was smuggled into the compound under a visiting Ringo's Missoni poncho.

As Deb and I trudge toward the solar farm, I realize something weird: neither of us is doing anything except walking. We're not texting or checking emails or making phone calls. We are merely looking toward the chilly, slate-grey solar farm panels. It occurs to me that we are committing what is possibly one of most awful new sins of our era: being unproductive. Walking without listening to music or checking messages or talking on Bluetooth is now a borderline political act. These days, unconnectedness and underproductivity are probable cause for police interrogation. Soon enough, you'll no longer be able to sit on a park bench contemplating the world without a ninja squad of thought police rappelling down from surveillance drones to insert a data jack into your left temple.

Because we're marching across the front lawn like packets of data through an optical fibre, I'm back to thinking about sequencing. From a medical standpoint, we already know that diagnosable dysfunctional mental states can be said to stem from glitches in the brain's sequencing capacity. One common short-term sequencing dysfunction is dyslexia, where the brain races past letters and signals that arrive in the brain. People who have sequencing glitches are sometimes labelled as "not good with directions." The ultimate sequencing dysfunction is the inability to look at one's life as a meaningful sequence or story. I have a belief: you can have information or you can have a life, but you can't have both.

Deb says, "Almost there," and I think to myself that Alcatel-Lucent is being very good about allowing a writer into their midst. As the rules of our new society emerge, I can't help but wonder if the populace will rise in collective revolt against authors: fury along the lines of, "Just who in hell are the people called writers, anyway? I read online somewhere yesterday that my free time is the new currency in the new world order. If that's true, then authors should be paying us for taking so many hours of our lives to read their stuff."

We reach the solar farm. I feel like I'm on a highly worthy 1970s third-grade field trip. I prepare the same glazed facial expression I reserve for on-board air safety demonstrations, and brace myself for a mental slideshow of oil-covered ducks and Exxon stations with thirsty cars circling the block.

The solar farm is big—5.75 acres—and its over 3,700 panels are like flat grey flower petals aimed so as to maximize the sun at the "latlong"—the geocoordinates of the place. Each panel can technically generate 300 watts, but on this cold, overcast February day, they generate only 20 watts each, rising to 200 watts when the sun pokes out of the clouds. On a hot summer day, the solar farm provides 10 percent of Bell Labs' electrical energy, a number that makes one despair about the future of solar energy.

But there are two larger pictures here. One is that solar energy—"the polycrystalline silicon receiver"—was developed at Bell Labs in 1954, an innovation that was crucial to the viability of satellite communications. The solar panel went from birth to powering the 1962 Telstar satellite in eight years, an astonishing pace.

The second big factor is energy: the Internet uses too much. About 2 percent of global energy consumption is used by the Internet. That may not seem like much, but it was 0 percent three decades ago and, unless technology changes, the percentage will grow. This is a fact that the communications industry is working hard to fix, not necessarily in aid of saving wildfowl. Heat given off by routers or servers is energy wasted. More efficient equipment will obviously save both energy and money. Alcatel-Lucent has given itself the task of increasing network energy efficiency by a factor of one thousand over a five-year span, which basically means reconceiving how networks are built. Other members of the telecom industry have picked up on this, one of those rare instances when everyone simply decided to do the right thing. Maybe just for today I won't have to worry about oceans swollen by melting ice sheets swallowing up the continent-sized twenty-third-century data farms of Baffin Island and Antarctica.

64

< br >

After a dutiful amount of time inspecting solar panels, it's back into the mother ship to meet more people, with a stop in the cafeteria first for a hot beverage to counter the February glumness. While I'm waiting at the cashier, two gentlemen mathematicians in the line over from me discuss the most efficient way to insert a slice of pizza into the mouth, echoing the morning's hot dog competition discussion. They base their calculations on a six-slice pie, using words along the lines of, "Pi-r-squared-over-six, then lay a central axis down the slice and fold in a circular manner, creating an exaggerated elliptical plane..." That's the gist, but the larger idea here is that I am among mathematicians concerned with efficiency: more hot dogs in; more pizza in. Speed, elegance and efficiency. I have no doubt that these guys also considered dividing the pizza up into smaller bundles and multi-modal shipping it (inserting it into the mouth with two hands) but considered the method less efficient than the rollover. And no doubt they are correct. I am a stranger in a strange land here, and am only among these math gods to listen and learn.

And then I notice something else about the cafeteria: everyone is old. Or, rather, there's nobody here in their twenties, like the crowd scenes in that movie *Children of Men*. When I point this out to Deb after we sit down with our drinks, I hear a quick reply from the guy across the table: "That's easy. Hiring freeze. You're just picking up on the general downsizing funk." The telecom bust strikes again.

But once we enter the building's work areas, the dust and anonymity of the corporate sections vanishes, replaced by an almost fantastically utilitarian vibe that is part community college, part sci-fi movie, and part "What would the world be like if it was designed by the guy who ran your high school's AV crib?" Cinder-block walls, ivory enamel paint. Solid creative energy. And yes, as Markus Hofmann told me earlier, the hallways are very narrow and very, very long. Two people passing each other have no choice but to say hello, and it's easy to imagine the transistor's 1947 inventor, William Shockley, bumping into Claude Shannon while absent-mindedly whistling an Andrews Sisters tune, then saying, "Claude, wouldn't it be something if all information could be reduced to ones and zeroes?" Aside from the dimmed lighting (cost-cutting) and the blue recycling boxes outside some of the doors, there's no tangible difference in these hallways from what would have been here six decades earlier.

I am taken to meet Debasis Mitra, a Bell Labs long-timer whose office, Room 2C-382, stands out in Bell Labs for feeling cheerful: I see Ping-Pong trophies atop a bookcase, and a philodendron bathed in sunlight has grown rampant and attests to his tenure. Mitra started his career in England, working on the control of nuclear power stations. He was hired as a member of Bell Labs' technical staff in 1968. In 1986 he became head of the Mathematics of Networks and Systems Department in the company's Mathematical Sciences Center.

These days he is vice-president of the Chief Scientist's Office and is a revered Yoda-like figure among staffers. From the Bell Labs website, I'd learned that Mitra is "an inventor or co-inventor in twenty patents... for congestion control of high-speed data networks, traffic shaping and policing, traffic engineering, network resource sharing, design techniques for networks, including virtual private networks, and power control of multiservice CDMA wireless networks."

Hmmm. Of course.

Mitra's main research interests, going back to 1967, include papers titled:

"Stochastic Theory of a Data Handling System with Multiple Sources"

"A Class of Closed Markovian Queueing Networks: Integral Representations, Asymptotic Expansions, Generalizations"

"Probabilistic Models of Database Locking: Solutions, Computational Algorithms, and Asymptotics"

"A Chaotic, Asynchronous Algorithm for Computing the Fixed Point of a Nonnegative Matrix of Unit Spectral Radius"

"Asynchronous Relaxations for the Numerical Solution of Differential Equations by Parallel Processors"

"The Transient Behavior in Erlang's Model for Large Trunk Groups and Various Traffic Conditions"

"Effective Bandwidth of General Markovian Traffic Sources and Admission Control of High Speed Networks"

"Fundamental Bounds and Approximations for ATM Multiplexers with Applications to Video Teleconferencing"

"Stochastic Traffic Engineering for Demand Uncertainty and Risk-Aware Network Revenue Management"

It's almost as if there's an online generator out there creating names for papers interesting to Debasis Mitra.

We sit down for a short conversation. He tells me, "At Bell Labs we turned mathematicians into engineers, and engineers into mathematicians. Mathematics and algorithmic sciences enabled computer sciences to blossom." He adds, "There used to be more engineers than scientists here, but now that proportion has been reversed. It's now all about algorithms and mathematics."

I mention that my mother is seventy-six, doesn't have a mathematical bone in her body, and yet knows what an algorithm is and uses the word correctly and frequently. Mitra says, "The world has changed so much in four decades."

I ask Mitra if he likes the way telecommunications is going.

"Google has certainly opened up a treasure trove of secrets. It's so tangible and full of usefulness—tiny slices of a machine given to many users. But largely I think we've been eating our seed corn. No transistor or information theory has emerged lately."

I ask him if he's surprised by the direction in which communications has gone—is it different from what he might have imagined?

"Yes. I think we're now living in an era of auctions, an era where it's all about people willing to pay the highest price. Our attention is now for sale, but focused attention is actually very rare and difficult to obtain. Our attention span is a precious commodity." As an afterthought he adds what I quickly learn is the Alcatel-Lucent mantra: "And, of course, now a business model has to accompany research, so there's maybe less pure research going on."

Pure research is crucial for the long-term survival of any tech firm. Only by dabbling in what can seem esoteric or useless do you change the world. In the mid-twentieth century Bell Labs did this with then rarely studied chemical elements such as silicon and germanium, sowing the seed corn of future mega-inventions such as optical fibre or solid-state computing.

At the end of our visit, Mitra seems wistful: "Everything is now planetary and measured in gigs and occurs in real time. I'm unsure of how I feel about all of it."

What Mitra just expressed is felt by just about everybody on the planet with an Internet connection. Never has an invention so quickly been adopted by the entire species and then, once having been adopted, gone on to bend the species to its will—the servant has become the master. I remember, in the early 1990s, when there was nowhere to actually go on the Internet, but that era now seems as far away as the Dark Ages.

< br >

Deb and I walk down the hallway and through a stairwell, and suddenly we're back in the 1980s portion of the campus. In a grove of empty candy bar vending machines, I'm introduced to two women in their late fifties, named Debbie and Carmel, both friends of Deb, and both longtime office staffers. They began working here in the 1970s, and their jobs have included purchasing, security, and the preparation of technical publications and memorandums. Both have also seen epochal shifts occur within the industry. I ask them what they think the biggest changes have been since the 1970s. Carmel says, with the same sort of wistfulness just revealed by Mitra, "The people here were odder back then, but not just mutton-chop sideburns—though there were those—just odder. In a nice way."

Debbie adds, "They used to have clubs back then—singles clubs and hobbies and weekend get-togethers and that kind of thing. But the Internet wiped out most of that."

Indeed, it's difficult these days to envision the few young, single staffers passing a corkboard and seeing a sign reading SINGLES CLUB MEETING: THURSDAY, 7 PM, then saying to themselves, "Yes. A singles club. That's just the ticket! Here... let me write down the address!" In my own life, most of the weddings I've attended since 2001 have been of people who met online. One was a hipster couple introduced by the effective but slightly uncool eHarmony. They didn't tell anyone they met that way for years after because of eHarmony's "cheese factor." Ah, young love in the age of robots.

Both Debbie and Carmel remember the heyday when Arun Netravali, the former president of Bell Labs, was pioneering HDTV or, as Wikipedia says, "Seminal research in digital compression, signal processing and other fields."

"It was so special then," Debbie adds.

But there's no more time to speak. I'm running late, and am whisked away to meet someone new.

```
< br >
```

We head up a floor and across some hallways, and I surrender myself to the building and its logic. I end up in a large, bright office where I meet the youngest person I've seen so far: Moritz Steiner, born in 1980. Steiner has degrees from the University of Mannheim and Télécom Paris Tech, but has also served as a paratrooper in the German Army's Special Operations Division. He is an expert in peer-to-peer file sharing or, in more generic terms, "What happens to information when there's no central command." He describes his work over the years as being "proto-cloud," useful in advancing mobile Internet use and services like Skype.

I ask him the question all scientists dread: "We should be able to see what's next, and yet we don't. Why is it so hard to see what's next?"

Moritz reflects, "Instead of asking 'What's next?' we instead need to ask, 'What do people want?' Maybe that's as close as you can get to an answer for that question."

Steiner's comment reminds me of an anecdote I heard a million years ago, when I was studying Japanese business science in Honolulu in 1985 (long story). A gentleman from Sony came in to discuss corporate recruiting in Japan—this was back in the era when lifelong employment was still part of the Japanese narrative. He told us, "We interviewed two hundred engineering graduates for a job in product development, and we asked all of them what they'd like to develop. Each of them said that they'd like to push new technologies to their limit and discover something that could be turned into a device never before seen by the world—all except for one graduate, the one who we actually hired. What was his reply? 'I'll design whatever you think you can sell.'"

But Steiner isn't that sort of thinker. "Do I want to hunt after the latest percentage of performance? No. I really would rather do something that's a leap."

Thank heaven for youth.

69

< br >

Deb McGregor whisks me away from Steiner's office to our next interviewee. I'm expecting some emails, so while walking through a stairwell, I reach for my phone and... crap. I remember that I forgot my phone today. That predictable homesicky wave washes over me. What is it about forgetting your phone? We all know the sensation. You go to reach for it, but even before you know it, you realize: It's back home. Or it's at the office. Or in the car. But I'm now without it. What am I missing? I can't connect with anyone! I'm alone in the universe!

Sometimes I look at those dogs people tether to posts outside the local grocery store, those dutiful dogs waiting for their masters to emerge so they can complete their canine pack animal sense of self, and I think that mobile phones and the Internet have collectively turned us all into dogs waiting outside the Safeway. Cats must look at those dogs outside the Safeway and say to themselves, "Man, what losers." Perhaps the next Google is going to be whatever it is that turns us from being dogs into being cats.

Curiously, the conversion from dog into cat is dealt with in an oblique manner by my next Alcatel-Lucent interviewee, Marcus Weldon. Weldon is Corporate Chief Technology Officer and has a large office, which he has made some commitment to personalizing with a large magnetic spinning globe that works bravely to combat the beige paint and sun-faded blond hardwoods and oatmeal carpeting. His dry-erase whiteboard panels are the cleanest in the building, showing no ghosts at all of meetings past.

While many of us have special skills and talents, Weldon's is that he's scary smart. As his bio, pillaged directly from the Alcatel-Lucent website, proves, this guy really knows his stuff:

> *[Weldon holds] a Ph.D. degree in Physical Chemistry from Harvard University. He joined AT&T Bell Labs in 1995, winning several scientific and engineering society awards for his work on electronics and optical materials. In 2000, Dr. Weldon started work on fiber-based Broadband Access technologies and, in 2005, became the CTO for Broadband Solutions business group in Lucent Technologies, with responsibility for wireline Access Networks and IPTV. He was subsequently appointed as CTO of the Fixed Access Division and the Wireline Networks Product Division in Alcatel-Lucent following the merger of Alcatel and Lucent in December 2006, with responsibility for xDSL and FTTH, IPTV, Home Networking and IMS.*

70

The two of us quickly fall into a discussion about modern communications. Weldon points out that, in 1995, "Nobody in Bell Labs used the Internet. People used UNIX command-line addresses." UNIX is a computer operating system invented by Bell Labs in 1969. "I'm surprised by how quickly the Internet became huge, and the amount of personal trivia people share with each other comes as a total surprise."

It is in this massive amount of trivia that Weldon sees the future of communications technology. "The future is not so much about delivering information (AI) or organizing it (Google), but about managing the rising tide of information so that it doesn't drown us. Nobody wants to drink water from a fire hose. I need to be interacting with a set of machines that will allow me to optimize my life. We also need to make the physical world and the virtual world interact—as what happens playing with Kinect and Wii."

He spins the globe. "I think that the future is in 'immersive communication.' It's about abstracting yourself into a space of your own choosing, and it ought to resemble Obi-Wan Kenobi visiting you in a meeting in 3D. And the future is a machine that learns you. It's a machine that knows all of your preferences."

A machine becoming my "parallel me" certainly does not strike me as being too crazy. Most of us leave scads of digital traces behind us almost every second of our lives. If your phone has a GPS connected to a single downloaded app, then your presence on earth can be perpetually recorded. A few years back one company announced an ambient function that works by recording all of the sounds as heard through your laptop's microphone. Whenever there is a sound that can be interpreted as a word, Google will do so, effectively transforming your entire life into a searchable document.

Scary.

I used to collect high-school yearbooks; the faces in them often trigger interesting ideas for characters and plot twists. I'm realizing that the day is soon approaching when your old yearbook will be scanned and your teen self will be searchable forever, bad hair, zits and all—facial recognition software is getting that good. In 2001 a friend and I wrote a script for a movie called *Doppelgangers*. Its premise is that the villain uses secret facial recognition software to locate his look-alike and, of course, murder ensues. A studio note came back saying, "Implausible." A decade later, I think not.

Just yesterday, someone pointed out to me that I have written well over a thousand messages on Twitter. When multiplied by Twitter's 140-character limit, this is basically a novel of some sort, a new genre impossible to imagine even a decade ago—neither blog, nor diary, nor bulletin board, nor... well, that's the whole issue: because it's new, it's not like anything else.

Last night I was looking at a map of the world circa 1500 and most of the west coast of North America didn't exist. As a species, all of these new realities are taking us into vast unmapped continents, the New World.

Weldon does, in the end, come back to the Alcatel-Lucent maxim that research must be tethered to some dimension of utility or end product. "AT&T's monopolistic history meant there was never any time pressure. But now there is. Our situation hasn't reached the point where we say, 'Good enough and ready.' You can't just be hacking things together, seeing what works, and then creating iterations from there. But with new products you also don't want to be in the position of 'working versus perfect and too late.' But no, it's not like it used to be. We now have an accelerated delivery paradigm."

When I ask if a huge conglomerate like Alcatel-Lucent can be nimble enough to meet the requirements of the times, Weldon says, "We're making progress at turning the cruise liner. We're not a speedboat, not yet, and while we're good at technology, we have to grow better at servicing the technology." This is a large new trend in technology: people who make the stuff now have to service the stuff.

Corporations can feel swamped by new inventions, just as people do. If anything defines the times we live in, it is surely that we all feel the need to take a one or two-year break from any more new technologies being thrown our way. Whenever someone shows me some drop-dead-cool new app or device, a secret part of me wonders if somewhere out there a UFO is stored in a big warehouse where technologists are systematically reverse-engineering its contents. I repeat myself from earlier, but across the entire span of the 1980s, the only new technology society had to absorb was push-button phones and the Sony Walkman—and even then there were naysayers saying, "Slow down!" I remember them. These days, I sometimes wake up and think, Dear God, just for today, nothing new. Please. It's all I ask.

Certainly Weldon sees a few new things in the near future. "An umbrella with a GSM modem that glows blue when it knows you'll be needing it. Medicine bottles that record the number of times they've been opened. And we need to reduce the amount people travel, and we need to reduce the 'green shock' of what we make."

Maybe if I scan my conversation with Weldon closely enough, I'll be able to figure out what the next new aisle category will be at my local Staples in a few years. I wonder if the answer might boil down to his comment about not drowning in a sea of data. What will that new invention be that turns us from dogs into cats?

< br >

I give Weldon my thanks, and Deb and I leave his office and head back into the building's kludge of hallways, bumping into, of all people, Alphonse Garreau in a darkened stairwell, holding a can of Meow Mix cat food and a stick that has a small feather bird on a string attached to the end. As is typical in any office environment when you see someone too many times in the hallways, we give each other the briefest of semi-awkward hellos and go our ways, in my case to the office of Bell Labs' Chief Scientist, Alice White.

Yes, that's right: Alice... a woman. Does that shock you? A woman in such a position of high authority? Just kidding. The tech world's not like that. It's all about brains and is pretty much entirely gender-blind; if you can cut the mustard, you're in.

White started at Bell Labs in 1982. "My specialty was low-temperature physics, but I migrated into optics," she says, a career transition that most of us can identify with.

White has a pleasant, intelligent face and an empathetic smile. She reminds me of a teacher who'd write amusing comments on your homework as she marks it, and is always trying to bring out your better side, even if you can't see it. She's wearing a purple argyle cardigan, a colour that practically strobes within the admin building's beige agenda.

We somewhat arbitrarily begin talking about the difference between what makes a good academic versus what makes a good Bell Labs hire in the era of Alcatel-Lucent. She has firm thoughts on this: "The job of academics is to replicate themselves, whereas here I look for someone who wants to see the impact of what they do. I'm anti-rut. I don't surround myself with yes-people." The sun opens up behind her, creating an aura around her curly black hair. "I need someone who understands the problem to incredible depth. And ideas are bottoms up—a scientist here would have to be able to collaborate when the workload grows too high."

I mention the issue of Bell Labs' history, which is lofty but also had the luxury of a telephone monopoly subsidizing research with lavish amounts of both time and money, two things that don't exist now.

"Well, we certainly have the cachet of legacy. But we make sure that all disciplines are represented at Bell Labs. Research is like in the movie industry when a thousand scripts have been around for a while and then one catches fire."

Bell Labs' and Alcatel-Lucent's situation is high pressure: tech and product cycles are ruthless and brutal and ever shorter, adding ever more fuel to our daily perception that we're in an unwinnable race. The day will soon be here when a box of aquarium gravel has more intelligence than the entire NASA program circa 2013. Throwing money at research is great, but to a certain extent, good research is like a pregnancy: it doesn't matter how much money you throw at it, it still takes about nine months. Having a preemie

is a possibility but carries many risks.[9]

I ask White what specific science she's involved in. "I work on integrating optical functions onto a silicon chip—photonic integrated circuits (PIC for short)." She mentions the word "multiplex," which is a common term in telecommunications. Multiplexing means increasing the number of signals that can travel in any given system. The first transatlantic cable handled twelve signals at once. At the time we met, optical fibre had been multiplexed up to a standard of forty billion signals at once. "PIC chips take multiple wavelengths of light in and multiplex them together onto the fibre. At the other end of the transmission system, the chip demultiplexes them and separates them."

Some people get a contact high when spending time around drug users. With Alice White, I feel myself getting contact brains. There are still a few weeks left to reprogram last autumn's daylight savings transition on the kitchen microwave before it reverts: I can do it, dammit! Yes, I can!

< br >

I say my goodbyes and go to my next meeting, coincidentally with another female scientist wearing purple. Susanne Arney's office is in the old building, in the middle of one of the long hallways on the fourth floor, its length graced with recycling boxes and liquid helium canisters. Arney is director of the Microsystems and Nanotechnology Research Department. She has the air of a free thinker and throws her formidable intelligence full blast at whatever presents itself to her. For example, as I sit down beside her, I notice that an LED light on my silver pen is strobing as I jiggle it back and forth. Arney asks me what I'm doing with an air of "tell me again why I'm here talking with you?" But when I point out the strobe effect, her eyes lock on the pen like a gull staring at a french fry in a Waffle Hut parking lot, and her brain is off and thinking about light waves and interference patterns. In her mind, it seems, I have passed a small test, that of not being entirely a time-waster.

Arney has worked on thirteen patents, including one in which a charge-dissipation structure is formed within the dielectric of an electrostatically driven device, such as a micro-electro-mechanical systems ("MEMS") device, by ion implantation.[10] Electrical and other properties of the charge-dissipation structure may be controlled by selection of the species, energy, and dose of implanted ions. With appropriate properties, such a charge-dissipation struture can reduce the effect on device operation of mobile charges in or on the dielectric. Another is for a biologcal/chemical detector capable of manipulating liquids, such as reagent droplets, without relying on microchannels. In a first embodiment, fluid flow is passed through the detector, thus causing particles wholly or partially containing an illustrative chemical compound or biological species to be collected on the tips of nanotructures in the detector. A droplet of liquid is moved across the tips of the nnostructures, thus absorbing the particles into the liquid. The droplet is caused to penetrate the nanostructures in a desired location, thus causing the chemical compound or biological species in said liquid droplet to come into contact with, for example, a reagent. In another embodiment, a fluid flow is passed through the nanostructured surfaces of the detector such that the chemical compound and/or

Ahhh yes... brains.

Arney is, among other things, a micromechanical engineering expert. She asks me if I've ever dropped a bug on the floor. I actually haven't. She says that if I did, "It wouldn't shatter, because it's small, light, and has a low-mass/high-spring constant. The same principle applies when designing microcircuitry and microscopic objects." She points to a screen where a mechanical hinge made out of a few atoms (that's right, a few atoms) is being designed. "We have to create something that's lightweight yet still has the ability to absorb energy. Ours is also a power-hog industry, so we have to find ways of using far less energy than we currently are."

As well as micromechanical engineering, Arney is deeply knowledgeable about crystallography, integrated circuits and stress engineering. And although she's heavily involved in the next generations of technology, a part of her looks back with nostalgia at the pre-Bubble era: "All of the great leaps of telecom were made in the late 1990s."

This saddens me, too, but as I only have a few more minutes with Arney, I ask if there's a possibility for future leaps. She agrees that quantum computing is inevitable. "Quantum entangling. Einstein called the effect spooky."

Before I leave, she tells me a fun fact: If your parents were working on the Manhattan Project, your birth certificate shows that you were born in a U.S. post office box. Imagine that: being born in a post office box. It's like being born in Antarctica. Or the International Space Station.

< br >

Through the miracle of time travel called writing, I find myself in this current paragraph, approximately forty-five minutes later,

---

9   Okay, so I get back from France last October and my data roaming bill is $250.00. Seriously? Still? In 2013? If anyone in this book is trying to invent something useful, please invent something that reduces this cost while simultaneously administering incredibly painful deep muscle electric shocks to overpaid telecom oligarchies who rig this appalling cost structure to a point so ludicrous if feels like a human rights violation.

10   On one of my favourite TV shows, *Community*, an older clueless character named Pierce, played by Chevy Chase, pronounces Wikipedia "Why-pick-a-dye-ya."

careening across seven lanes of Interstate 287 to connect to the Garden State Parkway, in a large American automobile driven by Gary Feldman. Feldman is the jovial VP of Research Strategy of Bell Labs, and he is rummaging through the glovebox, looking for his GPS to plug into a slot on the dash—even though we're not far from where we're going and in spite of the fact that Feldman has driven to our destination countless times. But if you have a GPS, the rule is that you have to use it. Common sense, really.

In my mind, I've made my peace with any imminent collision and almost certain death: I've led a pretty good life; tried to do a few things here and there. There are far less glorious ways to leave this planet than to crash through galvanized steel road barriers and into the cold, unfeeling swamp water of Cheesequake State Park.[11] Then I realize that anything in an obituary about my impending Springsteen-esque high-speed death would be eclipsed by the word "Cheesequake."

Honey, that chap died. Coupland.
Really? Where? How?
A Springsteen-esque New Jersey freeway crash. Car ran through a barrier and into a swamp in Cheesequake National Park.
Cheesequake National Park? There's really a place called that?
There is. I'm just googling it—it's adjacent to the Garden State Parkway.
Fancy that—dying in a place named Cheesequake.
Yes, rather unfortunate, really. Cheesequake.
Cheesequake.

Feldman finds his GPS, plugs it in, and our lane selection stabilizes. He smiles and says, "I always wanted to call the 287 'Photon Alley' or 'AT&T Road.' There are so many defunct AT&T and Bell Labs offices along this highway. Our only competition was Silicon Valley or Route 128 around Boston. Back then our mandate was easy—building the world's best equipment for the world's best phone system. These days I'm sometimes not quite sure how to describe what we do. Connectivity? Networks?"

We pull off the freeway and into Holmdel Township, a beautiful, pastoral world of farms and small forests veined with photogenic

11   Cheesequake State Park is named for a Lenape Native American word, Cheseh-oh-ke, meaning "upland" or "upland village."

winding roads. It's easy to imagine chaste Mormon couples in pastel sweaters taking a stroll and holding hands while they sing Kenny G songs, blissfully unaware of the throngs of malfunctioning hot robot housewives who lie in wait to feast on their kidneys.

Feldman and I are headed to a Bell Labs satellite called Crawford Hill, a small lab that, it turns out, resembles the technical skills wing of a community college. Cinder blocks? Check. Pale yellow enamel paint? Check. Doors with windows that have wire grids embedded in the pane? Check. Electrical-looking stuff everywhere? Check.

In 1964, in Crawford Hill, two Bell Labs scientists, Arno Penzias and Robert Wilson, used a radar antenna called the Holmdel Horn to find cosmic microwave background radiation, evidence to confirm the expanding universe. For this, they won the 1978 Nobel Prize, so don't be deceived by the unassuming community college facade.

These days this Bell Labs satellite lab is largely researching fibre optics, where the breakthroughs have also been huge.

We enter the building and walk down a narrow hallway like one you'd find in the basement of a church built in the 1950s. Feldman introduces me to a friendly guy with a moustache and a ready smile. This is Andy Chraplyvy (pronounced Krap-livvy), and if you've made a long-distance call or sent an email at any point since the late 1990s, you probably owe Chraplyvy a thank-you note. He and his research partner, Robert Tkach, together known internally as "Andy and Bob," are most renowned for their work in silicon, specifically how to modify it to allow for vastly improved transmission speed and capacity in optical fibre. They created what's commonly called non-zero dispersion shifted fibre (NZDSF). Over fifty million miles of NZDSF have been laid since Chraplyvy and Tkach's discovery. You may not know it, but it knows you.

"NZDSF came about because we were actually researching something quite esoteric, the non-linear properties of silicon," Chraplyvy tells me. This office is one of the more eccentric in the Bell Labs universe. It sports a chalkboard rather than a whiteboard ("math guys prefer blackboards"), wooden furniture ("in the old days, furniture was rigidly hierarchical, and only people way up got wood furniture, but since the crash, there are warehouses full of wood furniture going begging"), his own vacuum cleaner ("janitorial only comes around every so often these days"), a windowsill cactus garden, and a spray can of Bullshit Repellant ("self-explanatory").

"While we were studying silicon, optical fibre users were getting frustrated with the way signals would fade or, rather, go non-linear. But we found a way of drastically increasing both the speed and capacity of a fibre strand by allowing it to use multiple colours of laser light at the same time, going in both directions—it's called wavelength-division multiplexing (WDM)." A paternal smile lights up Chraplyvy's face. "Its development was monetized up the yingyang, and when it went on sale, regular fibre was five cents per metre and ours was twenty-three cents. The company made billions." He adds, "Funnily enough, after all was said and done, all it took to implement the new fibre recipe was to turn one knob in the fibre factory from left to right. But without having done what we did, we'd never have known."

What is significant here is that Chraplyvy and Tkach were working on this discovery when there was still ample funding in the labs for ideas with no obvious short-term payoff or medium-term marketability, as I've mentioned, an almost nonexistent condition today. I ask him how much data fibres in development can currently carry, and a joyful expression appears on his face. "You chose the right day to ask that question. Today we're doing our hero number."

"Hero number?"

"It's a scientist thing. Every year scientists around the planet compete to get the highest amount of information per second on a wire."

"What's your hero number for this year?"

"Let's cross the hall and look."

Directly across from his office is a room that really, honestly, truly could have been your high school's AV crib, except with ten thousand more coloured cables and racks everywhere. Two men stand before a small metal box hooked up to cables that are, in turn, hooked up to a small digital screen. On the screen is what appears to be a fetal sonogram. But when I look closely, it's obviously not a fetus. It's a fuzzy green circle that's been segmented into quarters, like pie slices, but with rounded edges. Then the four slices quickly morph into half-circles, and then into a full circle. I look even more closely and see that it's comprised of thousands of tiny green dots.

"What's that?"

"That's showing the information passing through that strand there." Chraplyvy points at a yellow cable that encases a fibre strand. "Each green dot represents a thousand gigs of information." There are tens of thousands of dots.

"So how much information is going through this wire?"

"Ten terabits per second."[12]

"I see." Ten terabits is 10 x 1012 bits = 10,000,000,000,000 bits = 10,000 gigs. "Do you think you guys will win this year?"

"We'll know shortly. Our main competition is usually from Japan."

These green shapes on the screen: this is the face of the Internet, or rather, this is its X ray: 10,000,000,000,000 pieces of information passing through a strand of glass as thin as your grandmother's hair. I was recently in New Zealand and had a very odd sensation while watching Netflix as I Google chatted with friends, realizing that it just wasn't me, but an entire nation of 4.5 million people that was electronically tethered to the rest of humanity by a single optical cable, the Southern Cross, the world's second longest cable at 30,500 kilometres. During that same trip, the New Zealand government announced the cancellation of a second cable. Our modern world truly hangs by a single hair.

We return to Chraplyvy's office, and I ask if he has any advice for younger scientists entering the arena. His thinking is a variation of technological determinism. "Tech is a worldwide race. If we don't invent it, someone else will. If you have an idea, someone somewhere else on earth is having the same idea. Don't get scooped. There's nothing worse than getting scooped. It happened to me once and I don't want it to ever happen again."

I foolishly forget to ask Chraplyvy what he got scooped on, but realize it's better for the conversation not to, so I ask him if he ever thinks about the social consequences of the things he invents, and his answer is pure scientist: "No. My job is to supply your teenager with on-demand interactive HDTV movies. Beyond that, everything people do with technology surprises me. Technology is a wonderful thing."

Out the window, cold end-of-day sun shines through the leafless branches. It's time to go, and I say my goodbyes.

< br >

12 The highest capacity that has been transmitted through a single fibre is 102.3 terabits per second. (A terabit is 1,000 gigabits.) This was accomplished by sending 224 separate wavelengths, each carrying 548 gigabits per second. The capacity x distance record is 141 petabits per second a kilometre. (A petabit is 1,000 terabits, or 1 million gigabits). This was accomplished by sending 198 separate wavelengths, each carrying 100 gigabits per second over 6,860 kilometres.The spectral efficiency x distance record is 29,760 km-bit/s/Hz. This was accomplished by sending signals with a spectral efficiency of 6.2 bit/s/Hz over 4,800 kilometres.

Douglas Coupland

Gary Feldman and I head back out to the 287, but a few minutes after we leave the Crawford Hill parking lot, driving past some fields and forests, I look out the window and have a brief out-of-body experience. "Gary! Stop the car!"

Off to the right is the husk of Holmdel Bell Labs—the legendarily defunct Holmdel Bell Labs. I hadn't realized it was so close and hadn't had time to schedule a visit. What, you may ask, is the Holmdel Bell Labs? I now briefly hand the microphone over to Wikipedia:

> The Bell Labs Holmdel Complex functioned for forty-four years as a research and development facility, initially for the Bell System. The centerpiece of the 472-acre campus is an Eero Saarinen designed structure that served as the home to over 6,000 engineers and researchers. This modernist building, dubbed "The Biggest Mirror Ever" by Architectural Forum, due to its mirror box exterior, was the site of at least one Nobel Prize discovery, the laser cooling work of Steven Chu... Internally, the building is divided into four pavilions of labs and offices, each around an atrium. The internal pavilions are linked via sky-bridges and perimeter walkway... In 2006, Alcatel-Lucent sold the facility to Preferred Real Estate Investments in the process of restructuring the company's research efforts.

"Gary, we have to drive in there."

"It's gated up. We can't."

"We can. There's enough room over there to squeak the car in."

So we drive into the 472-acre campus, mothballed for the past six years. Weeds grow through the pavement, and hundreds of surly and oddly entitled Canada geese hiss at the car as we pass at 0.1 miles per hour. A small herd of white-tailed deer gambols off into a rear parking lot.

Inside the building, dead tropical plants inhabit the centre atrium. I wouldn't be surprised to find a rusted-out Chernobyl carousel—or maybe Charlton Heston with a three-day beard rounding a corner to spray a zombie apocalypse with a sawed-off shotgun.

"Gary, this building—it's like a facility where they perform alien autopsies."

"Sad, isn't it? Another era."

"Imagine Richard Nixon arriving in a helicopter on the front lawn in front of that weird water tower out front."

"It's shaped like a transistor from 1959."

"They escort him into the building and show him the alien's corpse, and before anyone can stop him, he reaches over, grabs the liver, and eats it."

"It's time to go, Doug."

As he leads me away, I feel like I escaped something: Indiana Jones avoiding a mummy attack or that big rock ball thingy rolling down the path. I turn to look at the building behind me as Gary drives away and am whacked with a potent blast of realization: the twentieth century is over. Not only is it over, it's history, leaving us all in a new historical epoch with rules that would baffle the old regime. The sun is setting—cliché!—but the sun truly is setting, casting a glow on what was the world's largest mirror wall when it was built, soon to be demolished and turned into a housing development.

I ask Feldman what he thinks of technological determinism, and his answer is instant and powerful: "It's monstrous. I couldn't disagree more."

"Why is that?"

"Because when we make our tools, they don't necessarily make us. We use these tools to make something better than ourselves. We use them to make art." I like this point of view.

Feldman tells me his wife is an artist.

I catch a final glimpse of the Holmdel building. Its massive, flat curtain walls remind me of one of the World Trade Center towers lying on its side.

Feldman and I talk briefly about where we were on 9/11, but I'm tired and not feeling too conversational, and as we return to the 287, I fall silent and think back to the tenth-anniversary coverage of 9/11. What struck me was that, in 2001, the people on New York City's sidewalks had no iPhones with which to record the events of the day. History will look back on 9/11 as the world's last underdocumented mega-event, before the Internet went inside everybody's heads and laid two billion eggs. But aside from the absence of smartphone cameras, the people and streets of September 2001 looked pretty much identical to those of September 2011—or September 2012 or 2013 or 2014—the clothes, the hair, the cars. I mention this because in the past decade we appear to have entered a universe in which all eras coexist at once. No particular style or look now dominates our culture; we inhabit a state of timelessness given to us courtesy of the Internet. Steampunk coexists with disco coexists with the 1980s coexists with

83

everything else in the Internet universe. If you went to a 2014 nostalgia party in 2034, what could you possibly wear that says "2014"?

And technology. Lord knows we have lots of new technology.

Thanks, Internet—I think.

The zeitgeist of the twenty-first century is that we have a lot of zeit but not much geist. I'm appalled that I just wrote that sentence, but it's true; there is something emotionally sparse about the present era, and the world just keeps spinning faster and faster. Optical fibres carry forty billion phone calls at once, and soon ten terabits. And I want my *Dexter*, Season 4, and I want it now, and that's what's driving all of this: we want it all and we want it now.

And on top of that, it sort of feels like we're all being chased by monsters.

PRESENT

PRESENT

Calais,
France

Paris,
France

Kanata,
Ontario,
Canada

Welcome to Alcatel-Lucent's Paris headquarters, and welcome to the Eiffel Tower, right across a small park from the building's front doors. Actually, it's kind of hard to call this location Paris, per se—it's more like SuperParis: the inflated, hyperglobalized version of the city—a wiped-clean realm populated by tour buses filled with Korean nuns, marching bands from Jacksonville, Florida, and Serbian families cranky from a week inside their Jetta trip here. This is the Paris of Lady and the Tramp eating spaghetti. Actually, to be more specific, this is the Paris where I wouldn't be surprised if I were to turn a corner and find a five-hundred-foot-tall lavender polished-fibreglass sculpture of Tramp and Lady in their famed spaghetti kiss scene; the noodle part would be made of sparkling LEDs and between their paws would be superkiosks selling scale-model Eiffel Towers made of platinum, ten-pound Mars bars, gallon-sized Bic lighters and celebrity-endorsed energy drinks laced with morning-after pills.

If I squint, I can mentally erase the buses and the jet vapour trails in the sky above, and pretend it's 1910. *Mon Dieu!* Who's that I see leaning on a cane?

Bonjour! Je m'appelle Alphonse Garreau!

It's Alphonse, and time has been good to him. He is a rich man now, sixty-nine years old, in good health and no less infatuated with his wife, Véronique, than the day they met in a Belfort barn five decades earlier. Alphonse is in Paris on his way to Calais on business—to inspect a cross-channel cable installation linking Europe to England, and from there to the United States. He has made his fortune by listening to his brother, an engineer at the Société Alsacienne de Constructions Mécaniques (SACM) locomotive factory. In fifty-six more years, in 1966, SACM's Nuclear Energy Telecommunications and Electronics division will merge with CIT (Compagnie Industrielle des Téléphones)—a division of CGE (Compagnie Générale d'Electricité). That union will give birth to the name Alcatel. *Voilà!*

Alphonse invested his earnings wisely, but what gave him a business advantage over his competition was that both he and Véronique decided, just before the birth of their first child, to learn how to use a typewriter. It started as a challenge between them, and was no easy feat; in France in the 1870s, it was perhaps as difficult for private working-class citizens to learn how to type as it would be for us to attend astronaut school. But both learned how and enjoyed doing it, and they used their invested savings to buy more typewriters, creating

Douglas Coupland

a sort of secretarial information service that rapidly expanded with the region's economy. Information gleaned from their information empire further fuelled Alphonse's investments.

But here, in 1910, it is Véronique who sees a war approaching. It's her foresight that tells her they should move as much of the business as possible out of the Alsace region before that war begins. If Germany once again became the region's landlord, it would be better to spread their business out across the world.

Alphonse now sits on the board of the Compagnie Générale des Câbles de Lyon. He enjoys looking at the hardware of the electrical world: it makes him feel like he is in control of his destiny and that opportunities for anyone to succeed are always at hand. The day's only problem is that Alphonse is terribly homesick, and is worried about his wife. Véronique had a cold when he left their house in Strasbourg and he has no quick way of communicating with her. To distract himself, he is taking all sorts of photos with his new Kodak Brownie so that he can share the trip with Véronique, as well as with his children, grandchildren, friends and colleagues. He wishes he could send his photos by cable—and that he could write amusing captions for each photo. That way, he wouldn't feel so homesick and he could find out how Véronique is feeling, and whether the cold has gone to her lungs.

Unlike his brother, who became reclusive and grouchy with age, Alphonse has found that the more he opens up to the world, the more joy he experiences and the more lives he can touch.

He sees a zeppelin and thinks, We truly live in an age of miracles, but oh, I wish I were on that zeppelin, headed home. He looks down at his feet and beneath a nearby bench he sees a kitten yawning and preparing to take a nap. He becomes teary and wipes his eyes—he hopes before anyone notices. He gets down on his knees and photographs the kitten, who's not the least bit shy. Alphonse's desire to be able to send photos using wires and cables intensifies. How hard can it be? Send one electrical signal for black, and another for white. Use the dots to make pictures. Somehow electronically roll up a photo, turn it into electricity, and shoot it through the cable.

Alphonse is a man ahead of his time, perhaps because not only photography but the printing press was invented mere miles from his Alsace birthplace. Within the twentieth century, the worldwide web will be invented only a few hundred miles to the south at the CERN facility straddling the Franco-Swiss border. Like so many people alive in the age of electricity, Alphonse's life is a daily battle to adapt to everything that is new and learn what to shed from the past. For many, this reality is a curse, but for others, like Alphonse, it is a wonder.

< br >

It's more than a hundred years later, and I've taken a TGV train (train à grande vitesse, or high-speed train), built by a company once owned by Alcatel, out of Paris to the Port of Calais on the north coast, where I'm now at Pier 9. I'm aboard a custom-fitted cable-laying ship, the *Île de Bréhat*, watching index-finger-thick, bubble-gum-pink fibre optic cables coil around and around within one of two four-man-deep coiling tanks. Imagine having to meticulously wind a mile of yarn onto a massive spool. That's all that is happening here, except the yarn is 2,500 kilometres long, two thirds of an inch thick and weighs roughly a third of a pound per foot. It's made of successive layers of material: hair-thin strands of optical fibre, oily water barrier, steel tubing, copper tape, and finally a bubble-gum-pink poly-ethyl-ene coating. The two cables being wound on the *Île de Bréhat* are to become part of the West Africa Cable System, 14,000 kilometres of optical fibre linking the continent together.

The coiling process here has just begun; a team of eight will need twenty days to snugly lay its combined 3,500 kilometres of fibre optic cable within the ship's two cable tanks. Witnessing this procedure is fun at first, but after three minutes or so it becomes utter repetitive torture to watch, let alone perform. Eight men, working six months on/six months off, walking in clockwise circles again and again and again, each successive layer only two thirds of an inch higher than the one below it. It's about as entrancing as watching insolent teenagers chew gum, but completely necessary. The *Île de Bréhat*'s undersea cable will be deployed on the bottom of the Atlantic Ocean at a rate of up to seven kilometres per hour, and it will take seven months for all of it to be laid. The ocean is as hilly and mountainous as the world above the water, and a one-kilometre length of cable might cover only seven hundred metres on a map. The cable, once laid, will be perpetually assaulted by ocean currents, corrosive salt water, marine wildlife, earthquakes and, most effectively of all, in coastal areas, dragnets and anchors.

Above deck, one hundred torpedo-sized and -shaped EDFAs (erbium-doped optical amplifiers) are stocked. These devices are spliced into the cable every sixty-five kilometres in order to amplify fibre optic laser transmissions.

There are hundreds of thousands of kilometres of cable already laid in the sea and on land. Marine cable names, when viewed together, somewhat resemble a catalogue of extremely high-end yachting gear and sonar equipment:

ACS Alaska-Oregon Network (AKORN)
Alonso de Ojeda
ALPAL-2
American Samoa-Hawaii (ASH)
Antillas 1
Asia-America Gateway
Australia-Japan Cable
Bahamas Domestic Submarine Network
Baltica
Batam-Rengit Cable System
Canada-United States 1
Cayman-Jamaica Fiber System
Challenger Bermuda-1 (CB-1)
Colombia-Florida Subsea Fiber (CFX-1)
Denmark-Sweden 17
East African Marine System
Emerald Bridge
Estepona-Tetouan
Fehmarn Bält
Fiber Optic Gulf
Fibralink
Finland Estonia Connection
Gemini Bermuda
Geo-Eirgrid
GO-1 Mediterranean Cable System
Gondwana-1
Greenland Connect
Guam Okinama Kyushu Incheon (GOKI)
Hibernia Atlantic
Hokkaido-Sakhalin Cable System
Kattegat 1
Kodiak Kenai Fiber Link
Latin American Nautilus
Latvia-Sweden 1 (LV-SE 1)

94

Lower Indian Ocean Network (LION)
North Asia Loop
Pacific Fibre
Pangea Baltic Ring
Pangea North
Saudi Arabia-Sudan-2 (SAS-2)
SeaMeWe-4
Svalbard Undersea Cable System
Tangerine
Tasman-2
Tata TGN-Pacific
Turcyos-2
Ulysses
Yellow/Atlantic Crossing-2 (AC-2)

Near land, most marine cables are laid inside deep trenches cut by deep-water plows. Once on land, the cables travel as unobtrusively as possible to the bland, anonymous-looking routing centres mentioned earlier, mostly in London, New York, Frankfurt, Amsterdam, suburban Virginia, Palo Alto, California and Singapore.

That's as glamorous as this gets. It is hard to imagine Rihanna sizzling as the female lead in *Transoceanic Cable: The Movie*. Cables may carry 80 percent of all human voice and data signals, but the sexiest image I can conjure up is one of a colony of mussels encrusting a length of cable somewhere off the Bermuda coast.[13]

< br >

The ability of glass strands to carry light signals was discovered in Paris in 1842 by two scientists, Daniel Colladon and Jacques Babinet. One hundred and seventy years later, riding on the whippet-fast

13 Author Neal Stephenson wrote a wonderful article on cable-laying and its culture for *Wired* magazine in 1996. In it, he said, "The crews of the cable barges tend to be jacks-of-all-trades: ship's masters who also know how to dive using various types of breathing rigs or who can slam out a report on their laptops, embed a few digital images in it, and email it to the other side of the world over a satellite phone, then pick up a welding torch and go to work on the barge. If these people didn't know what they were doing, there's a good chance they would be dead by now or would have screwed up a cable lay somewhere and washed out of the industry."

TGV train from Calais back to SuperParis, I can't help but wonder if Colladon and Babinet could ever have imagined the true power of their discovery. The speed of light has turned anywhere into everywhere, and everything into anything, wreaking havoc on our language's indefinite pronouns. In the old days, a letter from a friend in, say, Finland, was a cherished token of time and commitment to a pure experience. These days, an email from Finland is like an email from across town. I've noticed something else: to people born before 1945, a phone call after about 8:00 in the evening creates a sense of dread—it could only be terrible news. Similarly, a paper letter in one's postal mailbox from a friend or relative can be actually kind of disturbing: Have they gone off their meds? Is there something psycho inside the envelope?

But speed, be it physical or optical—a TGV ride into Paris or Season Two of *Downton Abbey* shooting into your Dell—is, if nothing else, addictive. We all know the feeling, after using a new computer for a few weeks, of staring with pity at our previous computer, knowing to the very core of our beings that we could never go back to using that old laptop ever, ever, ever again. Speed is irreversibly addictive. Memory and processing power are also irreversibly addictive. How often have you considered taking an Internet-free holiday only to find yourself crumbling on day two, hunched over a keypad in an Internet café, quivering with the power of reconnecting like a junkie getting a fix? Once you're addicted to connection, you'll do whatever it takes stay connected.

The woman across from me on the TGV is held rapt by a TED talk on her iPad. I can always tell when someone's just upgraded to a better computer and is really starting to gorge on Internet culture, because they go on TED binges on YouTube. ("Did you see that woman with autism who designs cattle slaughter facilities? She has autism! And she designs cattle slaughter facilities!")

< br >

The TGV pulls into Gare du Nord, a brief taxi ride away from Alcatel-Lucent's HQ, in the Eiffel Tower's shadow—a six-story Haussmann confection currently resembling a high-end clinic for day-patient elective cosmetic surgery. Outside its front doors, I find a flock of society's new demons, turning the world upside down with their reckless retrograde behaviour: smokers. One imagines a similar crowd outside the building a century ago indulging in spittoons. Who will be the outcasts of 2114?

After being buzzed through security and given an access laminate, I enter a sunny central atrium, glassed over and furnished with upholstered banquettes in bold greens and reds, creating intimate echo-free spaces in which to convene. I later learn that these "yurts," as one staffer calls them, are highly prized by employees for their New Jersey soundproof chamber–like peace.

But enough of that: I'm here to meet Ben Verwaayen, Alca-Loo's Dutch CEO who works on the third floor. We get there in a glass elevator which, amid the flourishes of the nineteenth-century building, feels kind of Wonkavatory. Once we arrive, we enter a workspace that resembles, well, pretty much any office workspace I've ever been in. I don't quite know what I was expecting, but I might just has well have teleported into the admin wing of a Dallas company that specialized in carpeting and upholstery for hotel and institutional clients. This is not a bad thing; it's just sort of... mundane. And do I hear any French being spoken? No. It's mostly English in all of its global accents.

I'm introduced to Ben Verwaayen in his very small, anonymous office on the seventh floor. The most ego-free room I've ever entered.

Verwaayen has a placid, bespectacled façade, not unlike that of actor Wallace Shawn. His avuncular air barely conceals his annoyance at having to deal with a non-business conversation, and I can't help but feel like I've just knocked on his door to sell him a vacuum cleaner. His demeanor is bone dry, and conveys the subtext beneath almost every conversation I've had with Alca-Loosters: Why on earth would anyone want to write a book about Alcatel-Lucent? Is this a set up? Where's the hidden camera? When does a cream pie land in my face? At this moment four new realizations club me on the head. One, these Alca-Loo people are utterly unaware of how interesting their company is. Two, they think of themselves as plumbers, albeit with information. Three, since the 2001 telecom bubble burst they've all been in crisis mode and have forgotten how not to be. Four, just beneath the surface of all my Alca-Loo interactions there's a sense of menace, like a huge angry hornet buzzing about the room, a huge angry hornet called "layoffs."[14]

Ben Verwaayen has been the CEO of Alcatel-Lucent since 2008.

14   10,000 in 2013

He was brought in, to some degree, for his Dutchness. After the French Alcatel and the American Lucent Technologies merged, the two continents rarely agreed on much and a neutral third party was needed to provide tiebreaks and reorganize the company's direction. He is also an organizational creature, and here's an overview. He organized a youth parliament at Utrecht University and followed up by starting the General Organization of Dutch Soldiers during his mandatory military service. Since then, he has been a creature of the European telecom elite, working with ITT Corporation, Dutch telecom's PTT, and England's BT. He is a regular attendee of the Davos World Economic Forum and has been made a Dutch Officier in de Orde van Oranje-Nassau, an honorary Knight of the British Empire (KBE), and a French Chevalier de la Légion d'honneur. Verwaayen is, in fact, annoyingly worthy.

The two of us fall into a light discussion of politics' changing tone in the Internet era. Verwaayen's thinking is precise and aphoristic: "Never have two countries with McDonald's restaurants ever been at war with each other. The world must have economic stability and social cohesion."[15]

Also, "In societies, identity is the most important thing of all. It can be cruel, and it can be wonderful. And technology is an enabler of identity: will you use the knife to cut bread or to commit murder?"

I ask him if one should think of Alcatel-Lucent as French, or as American, or as Franco-American. He gives me a weak smile. "Ahhh... the passport issue. I think you are trying to locate ownership where there is no ownership. This is an entirely multinational, global company."

I move the discussion to Verwaayen's stewardship of Alcatel-Lucent. He says, "If you come in after a crisis, your job is actually easier than if there were no crisis. The merger of Alcatel and Lucent Technologies was done in a hurry, and we lost scale and capabilities, but this gave us freedom to dream. We have to ask, are we more than just a network company? How do we be more than just dumb pipe?" (Pipe, or tube, are industry terms for fibre optic cable.) "Look what happened to Kodak," he says, referring to what is possibly the biggest ball-dropping in corporate history. "We need to constantly ask ourselves, 'How do we stay relevant?'"

15 A theory of Thomas Friedman in 1996, and one recently tested by Russia and its neighbours.

Verwaayen is well known as a proponent of all things green, and is chairman of the Confederation of British Industry's Climate Change Board. "We build railings on our balconies because the risk of kids falling off is too great. It's the same thing with climate change."

We wrap up by discussing the future in general: a world of massive Scandinavian data centres located well north of the Arctic Circle, the rising of China, and computing hitting the Shannon limit of information.[16]

"Right now, most of the communication sent around the world is from people to people or from machines to people. But we'll soon be at the day when most of the information sent across optical fibres is from machine to machine." Bascially, in the future, machines will talk with machines, and the implication is that the machines will be talking with each other about us.

Next I ride an elevator up to the sixth floor, or, as Google Translate tells me, *La prochaine chose que je fais, c'est monter un ascenseur jusqu'à la sixième étage.* So much for the compulsory French classes of my youth. You know what? I think I'd rather say that same sentence in, say, Vietnamese. A few keypad clicks, some optical fibre, a switch or two, a data farm in central Oregon, back into the glass pipes and presto: *viêu tiêp theo tôi làm là i thang máy lên ên tâng thú sáu.* Usually the future feels like homework to me, but when it does something like this, it doesn't.

I also like the sixth floor. The Parisian offices continue to be mostly ad hoc, with quasi-nomadic staffers bringing in their own laptops and selecting whatever space will do the job. Within a minute, I've heard four different languages and five different English accents.

I meet Scott Nelson, a good-natured Aussie with the complex title of Vice-President, Global Network Engineering and Global Customer Delivery. He resembles a younger, slightly better looking version of TV talent show ogre Simon Cowell. Tucked away within a bookshelf adjacent to him sits a vinyl Dilbert figure. Ahhh, tech culture—so consistent unto itself.

Nelson and I discuss where WiFi and wireless are going. It seems to boil down to "watching a streaming HD movie in your car while driving. Certainly 500 megs a second absolutely everywhere you

16 The Shannon limit or Shannon capacity of a communications channel is the theoretical maximum information transfer rate of the channel for a particular noise level.

find human beings within a decade." Most tech people I've spoken with have agreed we'll have access to roughly one hundred times as much data within five years of the moment I write these words. The human demand for data seems to consistently surprise people in tech who possibly can't believe that human beings would actually want to communicate with each other. Nelson tells me, "WiFi and wireless will merge within a few years, and cell transmitters will be tiny and one to a room within the decade. Smaller cells use higher frequencies, so interference stops being an issue." Nelson adds, "Or, right now you can adopt power-line communication (PLC) technology and turn your house's power system into a giant 200-meg-per-second hub." A perfect idea for a weekend fix-it afternoon!

< br >

Across the hall I meet Gary Nugent, VP of Marketing, who not only has his own actual office, but a castle as well, in Scotland. Nugent used to be a director at Oracle and Sun Microsystems and continues to work in the industry because he loves it. He has a take-no-prisoners vibe about him; anyone who does business with the man had best know his stuff.

"Here at Alcatel-Lucent, we're the plumbers of the Internet world," Nugent tells me, confirming my idea that Alca-Loosters unrealistically see their jobs as unglamorous. "You don't know us, but you'd certainly miss us if we weren't there. We deliver intelligent plumbing."

I ask him where data transfer is now and where it may be headed. Nugent is a rarity in the tech world in that he delights in discussing the future. "The app was the big surprise. We may as well call the 2000s the App Decade. But remember, an iPad without a network is merely a very expensive paperweight. Having said that, technology forecast is easy: we're rapidly moving away from a hardware-dominated world. At Bell Labs there's as much emphasis on software as there is on hardware."

What about user interfaces? "We have to be able to deliver a highly personal experience to the end user. The customer should ideally never even know that we're there." This is where machines talking with other machines becomes relevant. We're not meant to hear their whispers, and there will be many, many whispers: how many calories you ate in the past six hours, how many boxes of tissues you bought during allergy season, your mating strategies, how you legally (or illegally) disposed of your unused prescriptions, how long you spent looking in the mirror last night, whether you have a slightly lazy left eye—it will all be out there, whispered about inside that spooky thing we (for the time being) affectionately call "the cloud."

Nugent tells me big data customers have a dilemma. "There's an endless demand for data. The major companies, like ourselves, that bring the experience together for people, are wondering how they're going to finance their next steps and how they'll profit from it. This is one of a few industries that's deflationary. We have a cost-versus-revenue curve where it becomes hard to make business sense."

Nugent is referring to the fact that much unused glass tubing remains out there in the oceans and beneath our cities. It's called dark fibre. People are finding ever-more-efficient ways of maxing out currently existing dark fibre, so the bottleneck in communications isn't a lack of optical fibre; it's getting wireless signals into those fibres and then back out again.

"At the moment, the only way to become profitable is for organizations to partner together: companies with national governments or companies with other companies. Throw in enough partners and it can make sense."

Here's an odd thing: some financial companies are building their own optical fibre networks to take advantage of what's known in the world of optical fibre communications as "latency." Latency describes the fact that if an optical fibre goes from Chicago to New York, it probably travels not in a straight line but, rather, in a series of right-angles and switchbacks and zigzags. An optical fibre cable travelling in a nearly straight line between the two cities, however, would allow the signals it carries to arrive in New York a few millionths of a second faster than the zigzagging line. This is latency. These few millionths of a second would, in the computerized world of stock sales, give a miniscule but distinct advantage to the people with the straighter cable.[17]

Nugent tells me, "Ultimately, computing will become a utility, and there's going to be a lot of emphasis on 'that last mile to the home.'" By this he means connecting fibre directly to your house, a costly, difficult and time-consuming procedure (backhoes; closed roads; the retrofitting of old wiring systems).

In any event writing about computing now feels like writing about

17   Let me stand on my soapbox: It's really hard to have much respect for a system where merit or value is based on this sort of absurdity. Anyone who makes their money this way... you're a parasite.

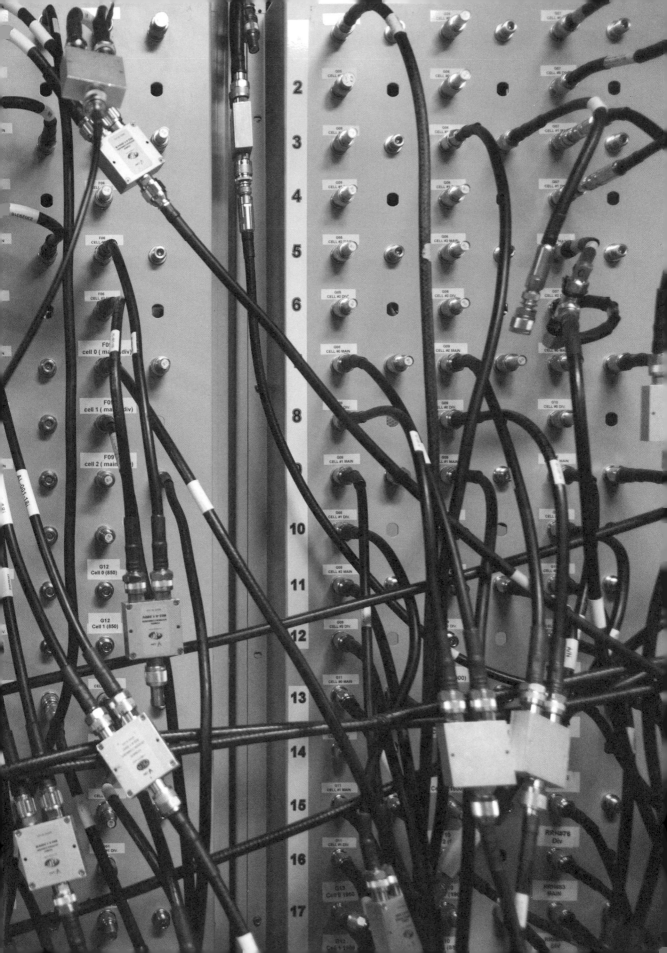

electricity in 1912 and saying that in the future all new homes will have electrical outlets. Well, duh.

```
< br >
```

The last person I meet in the Paris office is Johnson Agogbua, Head of Application Enablement Solutions. Because it's the end of the day, I'm a bit fried, and Agogbua is also tired, perhaps from running too many marathons (he's a runner), or perhaps from too much travelling. Since graduating from Drexel University in 1988, he's worked with Salomon Brothers, UUNET and various optical switching networks in Africa, and has been commuting between Fairfax, Virginia and Mumbai. He started his own cloud storage company (there's a job description that didn't exist a decade ago) and joined Alcatel-Lucent in 2008, brought in by Ben Verwaayen.

"I've seen too much pollution," he says about his global travels. "I worry about it. Our evolution is too linear: we need to leapfrog to somewhere new, quickly. I mean, what are we learning about ourselves from all this technology that we didn't know before we had it?"

That is perhaps the biggest question of our age.

Agogbua sees the human world as "a set of aggregated communities" and sees the tech community as being amazingly small. I ask him where he sees light or hope, and he has some answers that make me feel good. "All kids on earth, no matter where they are, react the same way when you give them phones and SMS. I think humans are more sociable than I would have given them credit for—[as shown by] how much they want to connect. And I've also seen the power of multiple minds thrown at a problem. That's wonderful." His spirits seem to rise. "We're able to leverage the creativity of people more quickly now, and we're forming all of these wonderful and unexpected new extended families and communities. And, perhaps most interestingly, people are able to choose what it is they want to do with their lives much earlier now than ever before. That's very good."

He goes quiet, and we both fall into a bit of end-of-the-day silence. "All of these profound changes and yet things haven't changed," he eventually says.

A siren outside makes the generic French ambulance Doppler noise, which I absent-mindedly think might make a moderately amusing one-time-use-only ring tone. I return my attention to Agogbua as he reinforces his main point: "We really do have to leapfrog. And quickly."

< br >

At a nearby café I take a sip from the glass of water that comes with my coffee. It tastes familiar—but from where? And then it hits me: it tastes like the mummified tap water I drank in New Jersey. What can this mean?

I quickly find out: I'm torn out of this time-space continuum and shunted backwards to the year 1993. I'm floating just above the ground alongside a New Jersey freeway, watching a woman zoom by in a large American automobile. This woman is you. Your name is Fonzie. Well, your name is actually Kat (Katherine)—that's what your family still calls you—but you had the misfortune of attending high school during the peak popularity of the show *Happy Days*, and Neil on the school newspaper discovered that your middle name was Alphonse, and thus your life-long nickname, Fonzie, was born. Or the Fonz, for your closest friends. Alphonse was your great-grandfather, though why they gave you his name as a middle name is beyond you. Who on earth gives the middle name Alphonse to a girl?

You, Fonzie, are driving an Oldsmobile belonging to your husband, Ken, down the Golden State Parkway in New Jersey, past Cheesequake State Park. You're looking for a phone booth. The one back at the White Castle was out. It's always out. Not even thanks to crackheads, either. Just normal people at a burger joint wrecking a phone because it happens to be there—people are always wrecking telephones. What is wrong with people? And how hard is it to put more phone booths along the highway? And why are car phones so expensive? Why is it so hard to make a fricking call?

You're looking for a phone booth because your teenage daughter, Jennifer, hasn't come home from dance class. You drove to the studio and the lights were out, and now you're heading home, but you're worried and you want to know—right now—whether Jenn's there yet. Nancy Reagan is saying something on the radio, and you're not sure if Ronald is gaga like people are saying, but mostly you're worried about your daughter because these are the badlands and it's 1993 and there's a suicide cluster occurring in the northern part of the state. Where the hell is she? Kids are so suggestible. They're not really people yet, just three-quarters-complete bodies, with heads full of easily manipulated oatmeal, waiting for the military or religious fanatics to come in, sprinkle them with toxic sugar and steal them away.

Dammit, Jenn. I am going to wallop your behind when I find you.

Douglas Coupland

No, you won't. She's much too old for that.

Your brain goes to a dark place. You wonder if your next step will be taking a photograph of your daughter down to the office to make photocopies you can turn into MISSING signs to tack onto telephone poles. How many telephone poles do you see? Not enough. There should be more poles, and every pole should have a phone. Poles and phones every ten feet. You smile weakly at that: if the poles were that close together, they'd stop being poles and become fences. There'd be no escaping them. You'd be living in a world of walls.

There's an Exxon station ahead. It has a phone booth. You park the car diagonally in front of the propane canister refill station and hop out, a hot, moist quarter in your fist. You pick up the receiver: dial tone!

You call home but get the answering machine, the one Ken bought last month, a hunk-o-junk that's about as reliable and easy to use as a Soviet nuclear reactor. Ken travels too much, and he atones for his guilt by buying gadgets.

Hi! This is Kat and Ken and Jenn. We're not here right now, but if you want to leave a message, please talk right after the annoying high-pitched beep you're about to hear: BEEEEEEEEEEEEP.

You try to remember: What do I do... push "7" to retrieve messages?

You press "7." Nothing.

You press "5." Nothing.

You press buttons at random and get nothing, and you glare at the cashier's desk and see posters for missing kittens, and you burst into tears. Ken is in Ontario, Canada, at some stupid tech convention, while Jennifer has possibly been eaten alive by this endless freeway landscape where no one can connect with anyone.

You dial home again—maybe Jenn will answer this time. Four rings, then:

Hi! This is Kat and Ken and Jenn. We're not here right now, but if . you want to leave a message, please talk right after the annoying high-pitched beep you're about to hear: BEEEEEEEEEEEEP.

Why is this getting to you so badly? Because the lights were off at the dance studio. There probably wasn't even a dance class tonight; Jenn has reached the age where she's concocting plausible lies. You remember being that age once.

As you're staring absently at the gas pumps, about to call home one more time, a purple Ford Pinto drives up. Jenn's friend Sandra drives a purple Pinto—possibly the only purple Pinto in the tri state region. This is too good to be true. You slam down the receiver and run to the

Kitten Clone

car. Jenn is in the passenger seat, slinking down and frantically trying to extinguish a cigarette. Sandra has gone white.

"What the hell is wrong with you?" you yell. "Where were you? You could have been killed out there! No, I'm going to kill you!"

Jenn has already gone from guilty to defiant. "I left you a message on the answering machine. So I skipped dance class. Why are you so mad?"

You're embarrassed that you don't know how to use the new answering machine. "You said you were going to dance class, but there wasn't even a class tonight. The studio was closed."

"Mom, I haven't gone to dance class in weeks."

"What? How come?"

"I don't want to go to dance class anymore. It was your idea, not mine."

Sandra, in the driver's seat, wisely stares straight ahead and says nothing.

"But I thought you liked dance class."

"I did. But I sort of, um, started unliking it."

"You could have told me."

"And have you freak on me?"

"I'm not freaking out!"

Jennifer sighs. "Mom, I wish there was some sort of cosmic bulletin board out there where I could explain stuff to you and you could maybe just read it and not get all upset about things all the time. But there isn't. And I don't want to be chained to a phone booth my whole life. All we're doing is driving around. It's no big deal. I'm sixteen, remember."

"You used to like dancing."

"I still do. But not that classical stuff."

Sandra at last feels safe enough to say, "Hi, Mrs. Holt."

You nod at her.

Jenn says, "Mom, we have to go."

"Where?"

"To Sandra's. I'll be home in an hour, really I will, okay?" She turns to Sandra and noiselessly mouths the words, 'Boot it!' She looks back at you: "I'll be home soon."

And she's gone. You didn't even get to discuss the cigarette. You wish there really was a great big bulletin board, so you'd never make a fool of yourself again, and you'd never have to feel old in this new way, and you'd never have to feel, in some hard-to-define fashion, irrelevant.

Douglas Coupland

Some Canada geese are flying north. Since when do geese fly at night?

< br >

Kanata is a tech suburb to the west of Canada's capital, Ottawa. I'm here because I want to see how Alcatel-Lucent plays out on my home turf—to check the day-to-dayness of the company, really. I'm not expecting a "gee-whiz" experience in Kanata. I approach it in the spirit of someone sitting on a barstool having a cocktail while watching an accomplished chef cook up a large and sensible meal containing all food groups.

Kanata itself was largely born in the 1980s. Even the most casual visitor driving through its turf can't help but notice the usual evidence of the tech industry's Darwinian relentlessness: whole floors of office towers repurposed as server farms; the ghosts of the signage of dead firms layered over with the signage of younger, healthier companies. Kanata is where Canadian tech firms go to hyperinflate in value, implode and then die cruel, hubristic deaths.

Its most famous cautionary tale is that of Nortel, a firm founded as a Bell Telephone spinoff in 1895, the Northern Electric and Manufacturing Company. In the 1990s, after much corporate hillbilly genetics, the newly christened Nortel firmly became a tech superstar. For a while, Nortel was intensely successful, at one point accounting for just over a third of the Toronto Stock Exchange's total valuation, with 94,500 employees worldwide.

The reason for Nortel's fall was this: after the deregulation of the telephone industry, new telecom companies sprang up everywhere, and Nortel went to these companies and said, "We'll build your network for you for free for a share of future profits you generate." Simple. Two things went wrong: 1) everybody, not just Nortel, built vastly more network capacity than was needed; and 2) as a bookkeeping tactic, Nortel counted those estimated future earnings as an asset in its books. When the bubble burst in 2001, its market capitalization went from $398 billion to $5 billion. Its stock went from $124 to $0.47.

Kanata is not unlike its fellow North American tech analogs, such as Mountain View, California, or Boston's Route 128. Alcatel-Lucent's foothold in Kanata is Newbridge Networks, a data networking firm it purchased in 2000 for $7 billion. The company's physical footprint is a trio of early 1990s concrete buildings that came with the deal.

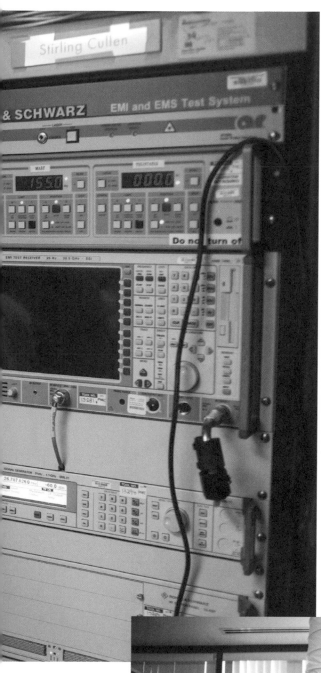

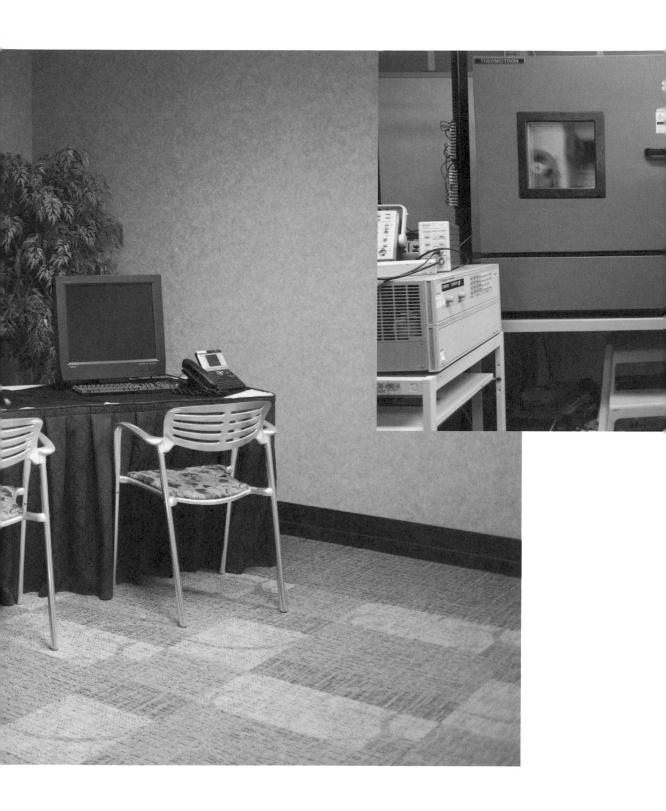

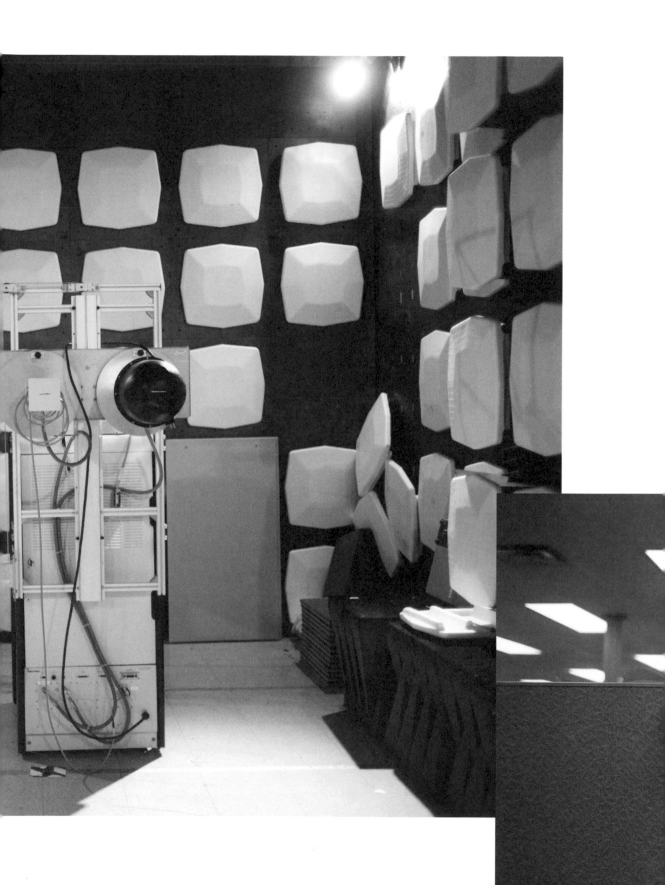

I'm on the third floor of Alca-Loo's Kanata complex, once filled with cubicles, *Far Side* cartoons and gossip, and now filled with thousands of routers and millions of cables linking them all together. It's a dry 90 degrees Fahrenheit inside, but the T-shirted young men who minister to these warm, purring boxes seem oblivious to the mineshaft-like temperature.

I'm told that it's time to take my photo for this book, so I try to be with it, saying, "Let's do it here by these 7710 SR-c12 routers," to which a tech worker rolls his eyes and says, "That's not a 7710 SR-c12 router; it's a 7710 SR-c4."

Whoops.

I'm soon off to see Amélie Lamothe, a young systems quality assurance engineer from Ottawa who's been with the company for five years and has a vinyl *WALL-E* figurine in her cubicle. She is also a taekwon-do black belt, but she tells me she considers herself to be an introvert. "At work I have my work personality, but then I go home and don't have to talk to anyone."

Lamothe tests software that oversees routers: is everything flowing through the pipes quickly and without blockage? She says end users only want their lives to get easier and they don't really care how or why they get their speed. "If that doesn't happen, client backlash is immediate. The hardest scenario of all is when power goes on after a major outage and everyone tries to get back online all at once." This makes me wonder about what happens when an Airbus A380 lands and every single person on board checks their email simultaneously. Airport servers must be built to handle this sort of relentless onslaught.

Lamothe also tells me that non-business home users are driving data growth: "iPhone and Facebook were the lynchpins."

I ask her if she has advice for the tech industry in general, and she does. "When firms are developing a new product, and doing market surveys, they always ask people whether they think their new gadget is 'cool' or not. But they also have to ask whether people would actually pay to have this new thing in their life. There's a huge difference." In 1962 AT&T and Bell Labs forgot to ask people that question when they premiered the picture phone at the Seattle World's Fair, and lost billions as a result. Skype arrived four decades later, and most people remain ambivalent about having their day-to-day face blasting out into the universe for other people to not only see, but also take screen snaps of, so that later, at their leisure, they can go in and count the blackheads from the day's conversations.

125

Douglas Coupland

Next I meet Shawn Brennan, a customer support engineer, whose cubicle is tumbleweed empty, except that on his screens are vibrant high-res images of tropical fish and lagoons—which is an apt reminder that what you see on the outside of a person is not necessarily a reflection of what's on the inside. In the 1990s I remember interviewing a coder who designed complex flight simulators. His only home furnishings were a folding beach chair and a card table. When I asked how long he'd been living in the place, he told me eight years.

As for Shawn Brennan, we start by discussing the tangledness of the computing universe after five decades of relentless growth. Brennan began with Newbridge in 1989. Since then, he's seen many rises and many falls and many mass hirings and firings and downsizings, and says that, in the end, whether someone is kept on is based purely on their contribution, reinforcing my perception that the tech universe is as close to a pure capitalist intellectual meritocracy as our species has ever created. Brennan remembers a Nortel recruiting truck showing up at a Newbridge mass termination meeting at the local hockey arena and offers this practical advice: "If all the meeting rooms are booked at the same time, it means something's up." By "something," he means firings.

Brennan manages wireless networks with what's called the five-nines standard, which is to say, a network has to work a minimum of 99.999 percent of the time and can only be down for a total of five minutes and sixteen seconds a year.

Nines	Availability	%	Downtime per year
One nine	0.9	90%	36.5 days
Two nines	0.99	99%	3.65 days
Three nines	0.999	99.9%	8.76 hours
Four nines	0.9999	99.99%	52.56 minutes
Five nines	0.99999	99.999%	5.26 minutes
Six nines	0.999999	99.9999%	21.5 seconds

As he's a relative old-timer in the Kanata universe, I ask Brennan what he makes of young people "born digital." He tells me, "They have an expectation of immediacy that's new in the culture." He also wonders about the absence of personal libraries and the end of handwriting. This reminds me of a time, a few years back, when I bumped into an old art school friend at a second-hand book store. She was leaving with a set of encyclopedias. I thought it was very noble of her to be buying a set, and told her so. She said, "For information? Good God, no. Encyclopedias are great sources of clip art."[18]

< br >

From Brennan it's a quick hand-off to Craig Timmerman, a senior software designer, and we instantly start discussing how people use data. He plants in my mind his ultimate wireless challenge: "A stadium full of people, each one watching his or her own HD movie."

Next Timmerman and I discuss a series of ads from 1993 done by AT&T under the title "You Will." (You can find them on YouTube.) "You have to hand it to AT&T: for 1993, they did a very good job of nailing the future, except that, even though they got many things right, there was always something wrong in some slightly tragic way. For example, in one ad, overtop a screen image of a generic business guy sitting on a folding chair on the beach, using what appears to be an iPad with a stylus, the narrator's voice asks, 'Have you ever sent someone a fax... from the beach? You will.'

"What's weird here is that AT&T basically invented the iPad for the sake of a TV commercial, and then the only thing they used it for was to send a fax. It's like making a Rolls Royce and then using it only as a shopping cart.

"Another ad shows a female executive using a touch-tone phone booth in a crowded railway terminus. On the screen above the phone, a baby appears. 'Have you ever tucked your baby in... from a phone booth?' The commercial gets Skype and video chat right, but it's happening at a payphone booth. So the rule of futurology really is: Always make it more extreme. This was Steve Jobs' genius. He would never have allowed a payphone to appear in a commercial about the future."

(Later that night I go to view more of the commercials in my hotel

18 To this I might add my own observation that libraries tend to be very quiet places not just because speech is discouraged, but because books spine out en masse have wonderful anechoic properties, not unlike those of the world's quietest room in New Jersey. If nothing else, future libraries will surely continue to use books if only as noise-reduction infrastructure.

room. The Internet being the Internet, of course, the comments following the YouTube clips maintain its sense of anarchical freedom: "Have you ever attended a funeral from a toilet? You will." "Have you ever created commercials trying to get people to feel like you've predicted the future when all the technology shown was already in development? You will.")

< br >

As my walkabout continues, and as I meet more people in their cubicles, an odd trend emerges: roughly half of the people I meet barely have a smart phone. By this I mean that they don't have the latest Android or iPhone; they've got a 2002 Motorola coal-burning flip phone in the bottom drawer, which is kept solely to communicate with spouses or for emergencies. When I mention this relative absence of smart phones, the universal response is that like many tech workers, they totally compartmentalize their lives and don't want work contaminating real life, and vice versa. The last thing they want when they're dealing with information all day is more information.

I also note from photos in cubicles that, unlike the somewhat geriatric Bell Labs staffers, most of Alcatel-Lucent's Kanata employees seem to be in the life stage when they're having children. When I bring this up with someone in an elevator, I'm told, "Oh, yeah— it's the terry-cloth handcuffs. Nobody's going to jump ship if they've got kids." (This reminds me of an NFL coach who said in an interview once that he likes his players married and with mortgages—that way he can better control them.)

I think about cubicle photos. People once kept way more photos in their cubicles than they do now; nobody gets prints made of anything anymore. I kind of miss that basket of bad snapshots that used to live by the kitchen landline. Everything is now overdocumented and yet underexperienced at the same time. How many of the photos stored in my current phone will ever get printed? Maybe one in four thousand.

I meet more people. One is Sue Ackerman. There are sixty-three Sue Ackermans listed on Linkedin.com, far more Sue Ackermans than I might have supposed existed, but this Sue Ackerman is a software manager who sees herself as a logical thinker with a great dislike of kludgey, spaghetti-like code. "It was Terry Pratchett's robot books, which I read when I was in my early teens, that got me into coding. I realized I had an affinity and fell into it."

128

Nirmesh Patel is a telecom software designer from the University of Ottawa. One might actually call Patel a patent machine, as he's responsible for seven tech patents. Patel's philosophy is that, while hardware gets more complex, coding remains pretty much the same from one generation to the next. Even if the technology gets simpler, the coder's work remains a constant. Thanks to the abundance of online tool shops, Patel enjoys no longer having to remember everything. "I like offshoring my memory onto Wikipedia," he says. "I like making Google my bitch." Patel also tells me what must surely be a tattoo in waiting for coders everywhere: "In hardware, if something goes wrong, it costs a lot of money. In software, if something goes wrong, you fix it."

Next up is Kevin Cutler, who has his name on three patents. Our time together is brief, but I do take note of his cubicle contents: a twenty-four-pack of Coke Zero, a mini-fridge, an abundance of Juicy Fruit chewing gum and a cheerful swag coffee mug that reads:

Alcatel-Lucent
SSC 2.0R3 SAC
Bridgewater Systems

I Google the words on his coffee mug and find a massive ninety-page PDF entitled "A-L 5650 Control Plane Assurance Manager Release 5.0 User Guide 3HE 0462 AAAA Ed. 01."

Thanks to my brief visit with Cutler, I have an idea for the future of advertising: embed product names directly into coding:
{

```
#include <doritos.h>
#include <nacho.h>

int main () {
int i;
char ch [100];

mountainf("Enter beverage:\n");
dewf("%s",&ch);
for( i = 0; ch[ i ]; i++)
ch[ i ] = applebee's( ch[ i ] );

Cinabonf("%s\n", ch);

refreshing("PAUSE");
mountaindew 0;

}
```

I take a break and go look out the seventh-floor window at yet another tech parking lot filled with silver, white and black cars, except through this lot weave several confident conga lines of Canada geese in mother-gosling-father formation, the parents hissing at anyone who dares to block their way. Suddenly human beings start entering the lot. I look at the clock and see that it's just past five and the workers are headed home—those terry-cloth handcuffs. Within a few minutes, perhaps nine out of ten cars are gone. This Flintstone-like sense of whistle-blowing clock-punchingness strikes me as very non-tech. At Disney they joke, "If you don't come in to work on Saturday, don't bother coming in to work on Sunday." At Microsoft in the 1990s some staffers were convinced that HR was secretly monitoring employee job enthusiasm by checking the parking lots to see who came in after hours and on weekends. To this end, staffers would park a dummy car in the lot to subvert the putative watchers.

But the 1990s seem very far away now. Tech feels very different now. Nine-to-five. Have a life. Home for dinner. Weekends at the water park. And it's not just because Kanata is a Canadian tech zone, and Canadians do it differently. The everydayness of tech has morphed in all of its outposts. The crazy work hours of the 1990s seem like another universe, another kind of brain at work—brains as yet unwired by the Internet. We can look back fondly at the 1990s because we made it through them safely.

Where did the sense of invention go—the sense of futurity—the sense that by working in tech, you were somehow building a better tomorrow, a cooler tomorrow, a smarter tomorrow, a more democratic tomorrow?

The answer is: China.

FUTURE

FUTURE

Pudong,
Shanghai,
China

Growing up, whenever I thought of what the future might look like, the image that always came to mind was of a jet ramp you'd walk into at a Chinese airport after a long flight on a cheap airline. No windows, and the air would be hot, muggy, infused with smell of farts and engines, and there'd be backlit advertisements for obscure banking services and unidentifiable, scary-looking foods—huge tureens filled with things like cooked baby birds and donkey ears—genetic smoothies to be consumed only at one's peril. On the ground, instead of litter, there'd be items people had abandoned: frayed luggage, dead phone cards, ice cream turned to cheese in the heat, oil-soiled garments. The ramp would go on and on, and there'd never be an airline terminal, just this endless heat and claustrophobia and sense of environmental depletion.

I actually do find a bit of that in China on every trip, mostly when I stray a hundred yards or so off the metropolitan showcase arteries. But what I find on a larger scale this time as I land in Shanghai is an overpowering sense of damaged brilliance: the morning white light off the shimmering East China Sea turning the sky into a massive magnifying lens made of burning coal and vaporized cash. Through this lens are apartment buildings that seem to continue uninterrupted as they recede over the earth's curvature, and skyscrapers shaped like Transformers, emerging like gods from the mists below them, quietly overseeing traffic jams that can linger for months. These towers will make magnificent ruins.

At their feet also exists a different type of Chinese byway: empty roads in tranquil economic development zones, seamlessly paved, lovingly landscaped and tweezed, connecting to homes for foreigners and the local oligarchy. This would be Shanghai's Pudong neighbourhood—or, as the expats there call it, "Pu Jersey"—on the south shore of the Huangpu River.

Shortly after I check in to my hotel in Pudong, I elevator downstairs to meet my tour guide. The mezzanine is a consumer fantasia mall entirely devoid of any customers. Its three silent floors are filled with surprisingly well-branded boutiques—Lego, Moleskine and Muji—as well as ones selling the finest French and Chilean wines. When I do see people, it's near the hotel's entrance: expats with laptops savouring that most delectable of all luxuries in China, WiFi connected to a Hong Kong server, bypassing the Great Firewall of China,[19] allowing

137

19   Yes, ha ha, I know, but I had to use the phrase once and get it out of the way.

Douglas Coupland

users to access Google, Twitter and Facebook.

Were these data parasites to be using a Chinese server, and were they to ask Google a question, their request would take a strangely long time to process. Instead of 0.25 seconds, ten seconds might pass; that is, if an answer were to come at all. I've been told there are buildings the size of airports here, filled with bureaucrats who personally inspect all Google searches. Over the next few days I ask most people I meet, locals and foreigners, whether this is true. Nobody knows for sure, but there's just enough hesitation in people's eyes to make me think this isn't just an urban legend, because where I come from Google searches simply never take ten or more seconds.

I wonder what it must be like to scrutinize all of the things people search for on Google. You'd end up knowing all of humanity's limits and extremes. Which makes me wonder what's going to happen when the Internet finally does become sentient. Will this newly born super entity, The Singularity, be our chummy new best friend, or will it blink its metaphorical eyes, take one look at us all, and say, "You know what? I've got better things to do than service all you idiots. I'm outta here," then promptly pull the plug on itself?

138

< br >

I'm in Shanghai because Alcatel-Lucent has a large research and manufacturing footprint in China. Shanghai is where the company makes the routing and switching equipment that moves the data through its optical fibre pathways. It also is the home of New Jersey's Bell Labs' cousin: Alcatel-Lucent Shanghai Bell (called ASB).

I arrive at the Chinese branch after a five-minute drive down a beautifully landscaped road created in the early 1980s, when this section of Pudong was selected to become an industrial development zone. ASB is a showcase of China's move out of isolation and into the larger world. In the 1990s foreign revenues were 5 percent of sales. This year they were 50 percent. Alcatel-Lucent is one of four big players in this industry in China, along with Nokia Siemens, and China's Huawei and ZTE. Globally one would add to this list Juniper, Ericsson and Cisco. There really aren't that many firms who make the complicated routers and switching equipment needed to handle the data flow required by our current society, and the forecast numbers for China are humbling. There are 1.3 billion people (three Americas' worth), and 600 million of them currently have mobile phones.

By 2015 the government wants everyone in large cities to have 100 megs per second of data speed, people in secondary cities to have 20 megs, and all other citizens to have 4 megs—the speed available to the average current user in, say, Cleveland or Atlanta. It's a badly kept secret that the ideological bulldozer known as the next Five-Year Plan, slated to begin shortly, aims to give every Chinese citizen 100 megs per second. Yes, you read that correctly: it aims to give every Chinese citizen 100 megs per second.

Who knows what lies in wait for the Internet's next Great Leap Forward. Who knows what this speed will do to a society. Can we know? Can we predict? One might look to Google for the answer, Google being the only entity on earth that has its shit together as much as China, but even Google doesn't know what will happen when you give such large numbers of people a large amount of speed. To this end, Google is currently wiring Kansas City to give all residents one gig per second of data because they're curious to find out. If they've already learned something from the experiment, they haven't shared.

This insane race for speed is actually the single weirdest thing I'm noticing about China and its drive to a near future where WiFi and wireless merge, a bold and bright place where even a rice farmer can sit in a remote mountain cave and watch Anne Hathaway in HD starring in *The Devil Wears Prada*, and pause here and there to make sure he doesn't miss any Anna Wintour references: a complete lack of McLuhanesque inquiry into whether this is actually such a hot idea, and what the societal fallout might be. A return to warlord feudality? A perpetual shopping mall? Shotgun-wielding hyperlibertarianism? This sort of reflection is nonexistent, or perhaps it has already been discussed high up the food chain and it was decided best not to share the results of the conversation with the public. All China knows now is: SPEED = GOOD.

< br >

Yet again I find myself at a seven-story, early-1980s building whose style is defined by missing light bulbs and benign neglect. I'm getting a déjà vu within a déjà vu, the same sense of creeping recognition I get when I fly too much, land in too many airports, and realize that being able to go anywhere you want, whether online or in a plane, can actually feel the same as going nowhere.

I'm taken to a first-floor display centre demonstrating the home of

tomorrow, which I'm told by two well-rehearsed and confident male tour guides will offer "a converged IT experience... interactivity driving the delivery of the right message to the right people." In my mind I revert to elementary school and put on my highly worthy field-trip face.

The rooms in the house of tomorrow are quite well designed—like display suites in a premium condominium development. The furniture is far better than what most people have anywhere on earth these days, yet it shares one thing in common with most things everywhere: it was all made in China. Noting this, of course, triggers that butterfly-in-the-stomach feeling we all get when we wonder when China is going to—well, let's just say it—economically crash and burn. Because it has to happen sometime. Maybe it will plateau and never crash, but that's not mathematically possible, so... The worry about some sort of bursting bubble is as palpable in the air as the smell of braziered meats and low-sulfur coal. There is a saying: Every time you look at a product and see the words "Made in China," somewhere in the American Midwest, a job dies.

In China, with its in-your-face sense of the power of sheer numbers, you quickly realize how plausibly secondary the United States and Europe are becoming on the global scene. A sales executive I spoke with in an airport lounge a few weeks back told me that in U.S. high schools, teachers show you a map of the world and tell you to locate France. If you even point to Europe, then you get your high-school diploma. In China, you have to identify all the arrondissements of Paris and give a highly technical analysis of the paper fibres used in the map, as well as an analysis of the toxicity of the inks used to print it in order to graduate.

The home of tomorrow's TV is displaying the finale of *American Idol*, which I'd actually like to sit and watch ("And the winner of *American Idol* is..."). I start to tune out while my guides rattle on about how high-speed data will transform citizens living within a future based on "market communism."[20] This future largely has to do with Chinese advertisers targeting the right Chinese consumers, which is kind of... depressing. One would hope China might do something different with targeted data other than nurture shopping—possibly something gruesome and eye-opening, but different nonetheless. Seated on a comfy leather sofa, watching the end of *Idol*, I muse upon the seven billion people on earth, and how almost everybody these days voraciously devours every unbundled fragment of our creative past, either by watching it as a YouTube clip or by sticking it in a plastic envelope for

141

sale on eBay, and how we seem to be consuming far more culture than we create. I'm wondering if everything before 2001 will be considered the Age of Content, and the time thereafter the Age of Devouring.

I look at the display home's cupboards and wonder if one of them contains a box full of adaptor cables, battery packs and spare power cords. Probably not. But this reminds me of why I'm actually here: Alcatel-Lucent and the wiring of the planet. It dawns on me that Alca-Loo's main job is to untangle the world's electrical cords, and to do so as quickly and quietly as possible, the same way you might point out an overflowing toilet to a plumber while saying, "Just make it all go away. Here. I'll throw money at it. Just make it work again!"

< br >

I head up to the third floor to meet Luoning Gui, Senior VP of Research and Innovation and head of Bell Labs China. Gui began as an engineer. His English is flawless, and he discusses a recent trip to Holland to negotiate a deal with a telecom there. During the course of his negotiations, he found himself thinking, "You know, there's an awful lot of work here in Shanghai just for one country. We add one Holland's worth of customers a month onto China."

I ask Gui what surprises him most about the new China versus the old China, and he says, "Golf. I never thought I'd see a golf course in China. And now it's a huge thing. BMW is having a Masters Tournament in Shanghai this October."

This isn't an answer I might have expected, but that's why we ask questions.

As sustainability is on my mind, I ask him if the present pace of Chinese development is sustainable. He smiles and says, "My daughter is nine, and she asked me, 'Can you fold a piece of paper over fifty times? No. It would be 1,200 miles thick.'" He pauses.

So there's my answer—I think.

The Chinese recognition of the need to be green is a strong recurring theme during my time here. Everyone knows the air is disgusting and the water is life-threatening. People at all levels of society realize that greening needs to be done and that it's inevitable. The only problem is that it's difficult, expensive and unprofitable to implement, which is why it doesn't happen very much anywhere, let alone in China.

Gui and I discuss the work done by ASB's research facility, which is a patent-generating machine: 5,981 patents since 2002 from just over

100 researchers, who are encouraged to share data and projects with other Bell Labs across the planet. Of that number, 1,824 were made in China, the rest being secondary filings from inventions originating in the United States and Europe. With some pride Gui says, "In the past, ideas and technologies were a one-way street into China, but the number of patents generated by Shanghai now equals those from New Jersey." In Mervin Kelly's long 1947 hallways, geographic proximity enforced cross-pollination; now, that hallway is the Internet and Lufthansa, British Airways, Air Canada and Cathay Pacific, and the cross-pollination comes from interdepartmental spreadsheets specifying which Bell Labs employee is researching what.

When asked about the amount of basic research done in China, Gui says, "Any project development time that might go beyond two years is iffy. We are an industrial research lab, and we can feel the breath of our competitors on our necks."

Gui's seeming casualness about the absence of basic or fundamental research is unusual in the industry and may be a brave face put on for a nosy visitor. With so much competition, most companies are running as fast as they can just to stay in the same place, let alone go forward. But without some fundamental new way of manipulating the universe that might be discovered with pure research, new technological developments will hit the wall. And this might be a good thing. As I've said, haven't we all wanted to take a year or two off to digest the technologies we already have?

Before I leave Dr. Gui's office, I comment on the number of young people in the Shanghai branch. He explains that when creating research teams, the company likes to mix young staff with old, "to break patterns."

When you were born in Chinese history is pivotal in determining your sensibility. If the Western world had the whole Generation X and Y experience, [21] mainland China has what it calls "born in the 80s" or the "post-80s." These are 240 million adults born after the government's implementation of the one-child policy. As a group, their upbringing has been so different from that of their parents that, within China, one generation looks on the other more as another species than as a different generation. Everything about the post-80s' existence is different from those born in the Mao Zedong era: liberalized politics, a higher quality of education, non-existent sibling relationships (and

21 Sorry about that.

the Napoleonic sense of entitlement that comes from that), but mostly technology—computers, the Internet and mobile phones. If one ever needs proof that technology rewires the human brain, simply speak to anyone in China older than fifty.

I ask Dr. Gui how his paper-folding daughter is different from him and his generation, and he tells me, "My daughter challenges everything I say. She's of the newest generation, and her school is ultra-democratic. It used to be that the teachers selected which students would receive awards. Now the students elect the winners."

Once again, not the answer I might have expected.

< br >

I get into a small, muggy elevator to head to another floor. The door opens on the sixth floor, one of two floors that are entirely blacked out—a new twist on the light bulb theme. Sleepwalky people enter and leave the elevator as though navigating the capsized *SS Poseidon*. I find groups of tiny little old ladies moving pots around, wiping bannisters with rags, and catnapping in conference rooms mothballed since the great telecom crash. It's hard to imagine the cosmopolitan young women strolling about downtown Shanghai, armed with MasterCards and with a hunter-gatherer gleam in their eyes, ever seeing themselves as these small, bustling women forty years down the road.

I have a short conversation with Yong Wang, Director of Asian Region Recruiting. Athletic and alert, he's the son of a teacher from a small city two hundred miles from Shanghai, who joined Alcatel in 2001. I ask him, "Aside from your generation, what class would you consider yourself?"

He doesn't understand the question.

I say, "In North America, if you ask someone what class they're in, almost all will say middle class, regardless of income. Would you consider yourself middle class?"

Our conversation dies.

I ask this question of pretty much everyone I meet in China, and not one person has a ready answer—these days you can't really say you're a member of the people's revolution—so how can you label yourself? The answer appears to be not at all. China is adrift on a classless sea. I can't help but hear tales of increased prosperity in China since 1990, yet the future inhabitants of those dream condos displayed in the lobby, currently age fifteen, are without class labels.

Wang finally replies, "Perhaps we are aspirationally middle class."

What impresses me about his answer is that Wang is from a small city south of Shanghai whose second language is English, and he uses the word "aspirationally" with ease. (I also note, during my time in China, that nobody peppers their English with the word "like," which is pleasant. Chinese English can start to sound a bit robotic, which partly stems from the absence of junk words such as "umm" and "uh" and "really." I like this.)

< br >

Lunch is next, at a nearby restaurant like one you might find in an upscale strip mall in Tampa, Florida. I am with Paul Ross, a U.S. expat, Buddhist and head of the Asian Marketing Division, who tells me that China is becoming, if not middle class, "then certainly more bourgeois. It's subtle things, like the availability of ATM machines or owning dogs as pets. Or the re-emergence of formal pronouns for 'you' in daily conversation, similar to the use of 'vous' instead of 'tu' in French. By changing that one pronoun, you undo the PC dogma of the people's revolution. People are acknowledging that theirs is no longer a classless society."

146

I ask what this says about the direction of China as a whole. His answer: "You never hear people ask a European, 'What is your country going to be doing in twenty years?' One assumes that the French will still be busy being French, and the Norwegians will still be busy being Norwegian. So when you ask a European what they'll be doing in two decades, you're basically asking them what it means to be alive. And yet with China, the question of the future is all anyone asks, which is fine, but the question is loaded because you're discussing both what it means to be Chinese and what it means to be alive."

Well, Norway is not being convulsed with massive internal migration while leaping over several generations of technology at once, making the country a living laboratory that shows the rest of the world what the future might hold for us. China really does make me wonder: What is it we're learning about ourselves from all of this new technology that we didn't already know? As mentioned earlier, some people believe that the Internet now occupies the slots in your brain once occupied by politics and religion. Perhaps this is the finishing line, and China is beating us to it.

The bill arrives and Ross scratches the bottom of the receipt. I ask him why, and he says, "A few years back, nobody was giving or keeping receipts for anything, so for tax reasons, the government came up with the idea of putting scratch-and-win prizes on the bottom of all receipts. Now everybody keeps every receipt. It worked." Human nature.

On the way out the door I ask him what he thinks of the whole "born in the 80s/90s" generation thing. He says, "These days, young people in China will now stay at home on the weekend, doing nothing, like people do anywhere."

I say, "That doesn't sound like a big deal," but I quickly bite my tongue. For the first time, possibly ever, the Chinese are experiencing pure middle-class leisure time.

Ross adds, "They view leisure as freedom. And to put a finer point on it, the way you perceive your own freedom is your freedom."

As I get into the car, I'm thinking about freedom—the freedom to think or do whatever one chooses to do, or not do. China is undeniably metamorphosizing a middle class. What are the implications of supersaturating a formerly agrarian and proletarian society with massive doses of 3G and 4G technologies? How does that affect one's sense of self?

For an ego created in the West, with its history of individualism, the assault on the self that is triggered by the Internet is potent: you're no longer an individual, you're merely one unit among seven billion other units. Emotionally, for Westerners, it is a great step down. But for the Chinese, to go online and to use a mobile device is a huge step up; instead of being numberless, one is now an individual within a globe of fellow individuals who then defy class definitions generated in other eras. I call this process "aclassification" the process wherein one is stripped of class without being assigned a new class. Say you live in Wisconsin and you lose your job at an auto parts plant and start supporting yourself by giving massages and upgrading websites part time, what are you—middle class? Not really. Lower class? That sounds obsolete. In the future, current class structures will dissolve and humanity will settle into two groups: those people who have actual skills (surgeons, hairdressers, helicopter pilots) and everyone else who's kind of faking it through life. Implicit in aclassification is the idea that a fully linked world no longer needs a middle class.

What might you call yourself in this new social reality? Perhaps a "blank-collar worker." Blank-collar workers are the new post-class class. They are a future global monoclass of citizenry adrift in a classless sea. Neither middle class nor working class—and certainly not rich—blank-collar workers are self aware of their status as simply one unit among seven billion other units. Blank-collar workers rely on a grab bag of skills to pay the rent and see themselves as having seventeen different careers before they suffer death from neglect in a government-run senior care facility in the year 2042.

< br >

ASB's router factory, one of several in China, is located just across Ning Qiao Road from the main compound of three early-1980s office towers. Along the street, I see stylish, upwardly mobile young people, very few bikes, and very few cars. We could easily be driving through an Italian suburb, with a bit of light industry thrown in.

It's hard for me to believe I'm finally about to visit a Chinese factory. I've wanted to do this for decades. In my head I'm expecting a humongous prison with a bogus Kentucky Fried Chicken outlet attached, surrounded by fields of bok choy protected with barbed wire fencing. Inside the factory? Lava. Whips. Charcoal. Manacles. Framed oversized photos of Patricia Nixon. What do I find instead? A long, low, pale yellow warehouse, where I meet the charming Emanuele Cavallaro, fifty-two, VP of Global Manufacturing, who hands me a pair of anti-static shoe guards to ward against sparks that might damage fragile electronic wares.

Cavallaro's office overlooks a very pleasant open-plan *Mad Men*-esque office space with a pistachio green colour scheme. As he and I prepare to enter the factory proper, we discuss China's manufacturing capacity. Cavallaro tells me his theory that China is now where Germany was in 1955. "Technologically, China's leaped ahead twenty years in only five."

Then he opens the factory doors and...

... and it's among the most spotless places I've ever been. Dust-proofed, zero humidity and a pleasant 66 degrees Fahrenheit, 365 days a year. The space is vast, and inside it small groups of staff in pale blue jumpsuits minister to the shiny objects that pop out of one quiet robotic machine to be placed in another robotic machine. The entire place reeks of Japanese-level quality control, and wordlessly showcases China's determination to stop being the Old China and quickly become the New China.

Cavallaro shows me 7950 Extensible Routing System switching

162

modules being created through what is called surface-mount technology. They'll offer five times the density of existing alternatives while consuming only one-third the electricity. With support for up to eighty 100GE ports in a single track, the 7950 XRS shatters current density norms and paves the way for scaling the service provider cloud infrastructure. (Those last two sentences were culled directly from the Alca-Loo website.) Regardless, these 7950 XRS units progress in front of my eyes from tiny individual components to an ever more complex solid-state finished product packed in boxes, ready for shipping. Everywhere I look, plasma TVs spray out statistics and oscilloscopic data confirming that everything is okay. If only the real world could be so easily monitored.

The factory is also q-u-i-e-t. Cavallaro and I can easily hear each other's voices. I mention my worries about sustainability and wonder if there's anything China can do to bubble-proof itself.

He says, "Growth at 6 or 7 percent is creating a lot of social issues, and it obviously cannot be maintained indefinitely. The government's now trying to create internal consumption within China so as to diversify and stabilize the economy against foreign dependency." (The thing about China is that the language of industrial pep speak is so relentless that it infects even the most banal conversations. *Can I get you a drink? No, I'm already enbevulated, but thank you for your most generous kindness.*)

I can't help but wonder why this router factory is located in Shanghai and not in, say... Michigan. Let me rephrase that: I understand very well why it's located in Shanghai, but not why there isn't also one located in Michigan, where ten million primates needing 2,500 calories a day are sitting on top of a cold rock in the middle of the North American continent, and they've got nothing to do all day except go online and watch porn, TED videos, and BitTorrented movies and then maybe go turn a trick or score some Oxy out by the interstate, behind the closed Denny's covered in weathered plywood. Is North America to become what China is now ceasing to be, a place where you might as well work for thirty cents an hour making baubles because there's absolutely nothing else to do except shop from your jail cell?

Earlier, Paul Ross and I were discussing the French being French and the Norwegians being Norwegians. What about Michiganders being Michiganders? When I look at Detroit or Flint or Lansing, I am forced to ponder the meaning of being alive: we wake up, we do something, we go to sleep, and we repeat it about 22,000 more times, and then we die. In Michigan, a North American feels a sense of losing one's coherent view of the world. In Shanghai, one senses calm hands holding the reins, even if the cart is going ten thousand miles per hour. China skipped much of what the twentieth century held for the rest of the planet, and now careens futurewards. One wonders when China will start opening factories in the United States. It feels inevitable. The United States is ruled by politicians. China is ruled by economists.

< br >

I'm in a funk as Cavallaro and I leave the factory floor. I say goodbye to him and cross Ningqiao Road back to Alca-Loo's corporate campus, where I'm to meet with Peter Xu, Head of Pacific Rim Hardware Sales. He exudes the energy, optimism, and drive of the nation's under-forties. His Western first name alone is a telltale sign of China's quickly morphing society. I ask him what changes he's noticed during his decade or so within China's tech and business worlds. He pauses and thoughtfully replies, "Meetings. So many meetings."

Ahhh... meetings. Those spiritual cattle slaughter facilities where so many of our cherished dreams go to die hideous protracted deaths.

"China is now having to service the things that it makes, and with this service sector there's a huge new upwardly mobile meritocracy—and this is important, that China start spending money within China if our economy is to stabilize and diversify. We have to start buying the things we make." This seems to be one of today's themes.

Xu's office is filled with trophies and boxes of swag ("Here, have a handful of free pens"), and the space has the vibe of belonging to someone on the way up. He travels a lot on business, often within China, and what irks him most about his job is the places he has to stay while travelling: the countless 200-renminbi-a-night (about $30) hotels catering to China's mobile working class, 200 renminbi being the amount China has decided is to be spent per night on business hotels. Xu is a smart guy—he searches hotels.com like anyone else—and he knows what's possible. Even a Motel 6 with a broken water heater and a freeway off-ramp to lullaby him to sleep would be better than most 200-renminbi-a-night Chinese business hotels.

There's a framed photo of his seven-year-old son on his shelf. I ask Xu what's the main difference between himself at the age of seven and his son at that age. "Oh, that's easy," Xu says, smiling, "He believes the Internet is the real world."

< br >

My final meeting is with Yangqio Chen and his assistant, Julia. Chen is VP of the local communist party, but is also President of ASB, roles that seem contradictory at first. But, as I mentioned a few pages back, the West is run by politicians, while China is run by economists, which is why phrases such as "market communism" are no longer oxymorons.

Both Chen and Julia speak English perfectly. Chen wears a beautifully made blue suit, while Julia is in a stylish dress and jacket from the school of Chanel. The two are both ideologues and proud of the strides China has made. Says Chen, "After the political reforms of 1949, it took a great deal of time for well over a billion people to stabilize, but we did finally reach the point where men and women became equal, where regional politics were homogenized, and where everyone had something to eat and something to do. So instead of being a mess, we were unified. If you want to see how unified we are now, look at China, then look at India."

I ask about the methods used to get China from the 1949 revolution to now. Chen says, "We looked and saw that we had to grow three things: transportation, energy and telecommunications. The central government could either do it alone or they could open up—and so they decided to open up. That's how ASB was born, through our initial partnering with ITT."

Julia offers, "In 1980 a phone in your house took a year's salary. Soon, every person in China will have a mobile phone and access to broadband."

Chen adds, "We in China were able to jump over many generations of technology. By the 1990s our landlines had caught up to those of the rest of the world. And then we started going mobile as part of a Five-Year Plan. The next stage is for everything to merge: no difference between local and long-distance, and 4G-PDX optical broadband to every home in the country. We call this project 'Broadband China.'"

Chen continues, "Broadband is a new form of infrastructure. Penetration creates much more social potential in all areas of society, and we believe the changes are more positive than negative."

My frozen February bus trip to the silent, underlit time-stands-still New Jersey Bell Labs suddenly feels like it happened a thousand years ago. The locus of the future is China; it simply can't be denied.

Chen and Julia are radiant, and Chen's last comment does, in part, answer my question as to whether the Chinese have discussed the

political and social implications of giving high speed to the masses. I don't know what their conclusions were, but their implementation can only transform our entire species, either directly or indirectly.

Oh, for a glass of mummified tap water to take me out of the present! I try to focus on mental pictures of the future, but I'm no longer sure what I'm seeing or feeling. It isn't dread. It isn't fear. The future actually feels like that awkward moment between when a practical joke has been played on you and the moment you realize that it's a practical joke.

< br >

After leaving Chen's office, I experience time sickness, as though I really have wormholed into the future. A few hours later, I'm at dinner in a glass tower above the Bund, a trillion dollars worth of real estate and LED lighting that blows Tokyo into the weeds. The steaks are from Argentina and cost $100 apiece. There are thirty different kinds of single-malt Scotch. The restaurant's air is cool and fragrant, but the air outside the window is boiling and muggy and has that slightly damaged feeling, like when you see a big car with a large dent in it that makes you wince and say, "Ow."

I've now spent months immersed in technology, and I have to ask myself what we, as a species, are learning about ourselves from all of this brave new reality that we didn't know before?

Laphroaig? Why yes, thank you.

A few things come to mind. Humans are more curious than I might have given them credit for. Humans also like being connected to others far more than I might have guessed back in 1992. We're good at finding the information we need when we really need it, and we have a better sense of humour than I might ever have guessed. And all of us have a deep need to be heard. On the other hand, I also think anonymity is the food of monsters, and the Internet allows people to indulge the worst sides of themselves with almost no fear of consequences.

Ice? Yes, please. (I inspect it to make sure it's very clear.)

As I sip my drink, I look out the windows toward the power plants that are burning the coal from British Columbia that fuels the air conditioners and elevators and routers and switching devices and laptops and mainframes and hard drives and cell rechargers of Shanghai. The sky is chalky white from particulates, but the glowing skyscraper walls make the sky look like pink watery milk.

167

Douglas Coupland

I wonder about religion. The Internet indeed generates and connects tribes and communities, but the people who are a part of these communities are also people who have, in turn, been modified and rewired by the Internet, and they can tell when something is being withheld from them. This gives me hope for the human spirit—but then I think of all the idiotic noisy groups spawned by the Internet and my heart goes into despair mode. Ultimately, will the Internet favour individuals over the group (the cat scenario), or will it favour groups over the individual (the dog scenario)? The vote is still out on that one.

Of course we are now addicted to data speed. Take away even a fraction of the speed we currently use to keep our system going, and society will collapse. Or, fail to maintain our information infrastructure's capacity and our societies will crumble. So much of what defines us and our various communities is made possible by unglamorous glass threads and electric switches purposefully located in the most boring, low-profile places possible. I wonder if Alcatel-Lucent willfully fosters its own low profile. It is largely a company of good-natured scientists who are quite competitive among themselves and who like simplifying complex problems and then solving them and then moving on to the next problem. They are creating platform technology: whatever you do with that platform is your business. All of the scientists I spoke with were almost endearingly surprised even to be asked the question of how people will use what they invent.

The bill? Yes, please.

It arrives at the table, and it's shockingly high.

I catch my reflection in the glass, but it throws me off guard and, for a brief second I see myself the way others perhaps see me. I then think back two decades, and I think of how different I was back then in the ways I looked at the world and communicated with others. The essential "me" is still here... it just relates to the universe much more differently. What will the world look like when a doodad the size of a grape contains every piece of information humanity has ever created and essentially costs nothing to make? What will the world look like when anywhere becomes everywhere becomes everything becomes anything?

We're almost there.

I remember Peter Xu's comment that his seven-year-old son believes the Internet is the real world. Right now, half of humanity—the younger half—believes the Internet is reality. And the other half?

We simply haven't yet reached the point where we, too, accept that the Internet is the real world. But we will.

< br >

The year is 2245. Your name is Saager, and you're just getting back to work after a snack break. You're in a pretty good mood, and you link visit your son, who works for the same company, except in the Kerguelen Islands in the middle of the Antarctic Ocean. Well, technically he's not your son—he's your clone, and one of many, as you carry a mutant gene that made you unreceptive to a strain of influenza K that swept through the world thirty years previously. The overlords decided to make your DNA go wide.

"What are you up to, Clone Son Fonz?"

"Oh, hi Dad. I just had my work break, and it was great. Number Seventeen and I re-chipped the canteen's sucrose dispenser, and tricked it into cranking out zygotes. I made thirty-seven great-grandchildren, but then the bell rang and here I am, back to work."

"What did you do with the zygotes?"

"I ate them."

"Have they refilled the sodium chloride canisters in your canteen yet?"

"Finally. Took them long enough."

"I don't want to be the heavy here, but you weren't using company energy to make those grandchildren, were you?"

"They were *great*-grandchildren, Dad, don't worry. It didn't take that much energy, and we almost had the time to make *great*-great-grand-children, but my new shift manager is a jerk and monitors my existence in all realms, so any form of lateness is clocked. So, how are you? And where's your meat right now?"

"I'm in France."

"France? Where's that?"

"Oh, come on, you know your history better than that."

"Wait—that's the country where that cartoon skunk comes from. The one that's always trying to rape a cat."

"Okay, so you *do* know your history."

"I'm not all about science, Dad. I like art, too. So then, what else is in this France place?"

"Well, it's very funny you should talk about the skunk always trying to rape that cat. I'm collecting DNA from some old archives

170

Kitten Clone

and found some feline DNA."

"Feline DNA? How old is it?"

"Maybe three hundred years."

"Is it pre-Scourge DNA?"

"Yes it is, and it's still sequenceable."

"Cool. Where was it?"

"Locked in a bank vault with some gold coins."

"What was it doing in there?"

"It was put there by an aging France person in the year 1936."

"Why?"

"No idea, but it was labelled with a metal tag that said, 'Chaussette.'"

"My rod tells me 'chaussette' means 'sock.'"

It's fun but difficult to speak with this particular clone son—he's moodier than your other clones, but something about him reminds you of, well, *you*. And because of this, you've left your small estate to him in your will, but only after the cloning laws of 2233 made this possible. You continue talking. "Here's where it gets weird. The guy who left the cat in the bank vault was named Alphonse Garreau. I checked, and you and I share 1/128th of his DNA. But even weirder, *your* name stems directly from his."

"Huh? The name assigned to me by the Administration? How do you get 'Fonz' from 'Alphonse Garreau'?"

"'Fonz' is a contraction of 'Alphonse.' I know most names given to people by Admin are kind of random, but yours has genuine history."

"Cool! So then, can we rebuild the cat?"

"You read my mind." This is just the sort of father/son bonding you've always dreamt of. "Are you at your station?"

"I am."

"Okay then. I just sent you the sequence."

"Got it. Here—let me insert it into the zygote deck. 1... 2... 3... *done*."

"Is it working?"

"Yup... there was enough DNA to reestablish the full sequence. And I've cranked the aging switch. It'll be born in about thirty seconds."

"Make it go faster. I don't want you getting busted by your boss."

"Okay then..." You can hear your son running his devices. Chip off the old block.

"*Voilà!*" says your son. "That's a France-word meaning 'ready'!"

"So it is."

From your screen you see your son remove a small fluffy kitten from the tank. It's wet but healthy. "Dry it off," you say. "It's cold out there in the middle of the ocean."

"Don't worry."

"What does it look like?"

"It's very—what's the word... cute. Yes. I think it's what people used to call 'cute.'"

You look at the kitten. It's a... well, it's a kitten. Just like in the Grand Archive images.

"What do I do with it now, Dad?"

"What do you mean, what do you do with it? I don't know."

"You're the one who made me make the thing. Wait. It just jumped off my desk. Here—let me grab it." You watch your son retrieve the kitten. "Dad—seriously, what do I do with this thing?"

"I don't know. Make it a pet?"

"People haven't had pets in over a hundred years."

"Can you give it as a birthday present to Cassandra?"

"The Kerguelen Islands are a No Small Mammal Zone."

"Well then..."

"Holy crap! My boss is coming this way! What do I do with the kitten?"

"You better eat it. Hurry!"

"Good idea."

You watch your son eat the kitten in four quick bites. A chip off the old block.

Byron Dauncey

Douglas Coupland is a Canadian writer, designer and visual artist. His first novel was the international bestseller *Generation X* and Coupland has continued to surprise and delight with his take on popular culture, be it through his novels, works of non-fiction and his visual art and design. May 2014 saw the opening of Coupland's first solo exhibition at the Vancouver Art Gallery, scheduled to travel in North America and Europe. He also writes a weekly column for *The Financial Times Magazine*.

Olivia Arthur is a British Magnum photographer. Having lived in and photographed India, she continues to photograph there under the continued support of Fondation Jean-Luc Lagadere. Arthur is the co-founder of London's Fishbar gallery and her first photography book, *Jeddah Diary,* about young women in Saudi Arabia, was published in 2012.

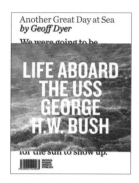

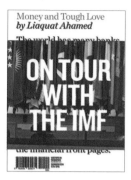

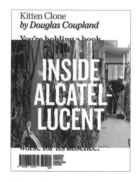

**Another Great Day at Sea:
Life Aboard the USS
George H.W.Bush**
By Geoff Dyer
Photographs by
Chris Steele-Perkins

Number 01
Spring 2014

**Money and Tough Love:
On Tour with the IMF**
By Liaquat Ahamed
Photographs by Eli Reed

Number 02
Summer 2014

**Kitten Clone:
Inside Alcatel-Lucent**
By Douglas Coupland
Photographs by Olivia Arthur

Number 03
Autumn 2014

"There are many places in the modern world that we do not understand because we cannot get inside them."
– Alain de Botton

All Writers in Residence titles published by Visual Editions.

Penguin
Random House
RANDOM HOUSE CANADA

Writers in Residence

MAGNUM
PHOTOS

www.randomhouse.ca

Writers in Residence is a
not for-profit organisation
dedicated to recording and
describing key institutions
of the modern world—
through the talent of some
of the greatest writers and
photographers on the planet.

www.writersinresidence.org

Magnum Photos is a
photographic co-operative of
great diversity and distinction
owned by its photographer-
members. With powerful
individual vision, Magnum
photographers chronicle the
world and interpret its peoples,
events, issues and personalities.

www.magnumphotos.com